Theory and Practice

Theory and Practice

Bite-Sized Activities for Teaching Reading Skills

Aviva Katzenell

University of Michigan Press
Ann Arbor

Published in the United States of America by the
University of Michigan Press
Manufactured in the United States of America
Printed on acid-free paper

ISBN 978-0-472-03942-5 (print)
ISBN 978-0-472-22135-6 (e-book)

ACKNOWLEDGMENTS

Thank you first and foremost to Katie LaPlant, my editor from University of Michigan Press; her patience and support brought this project to fruition. Thank you to Karen Taylor from colorvowel.com; her inspirational Color Vowel® methodology and sheer delight at the manner and articulation of language made me think, and think again! Many thanks to my wonderful colleagues at the Intensive English Institute at Florida Atlantic University: their generosity of spirit, collegiality, and professionalism paved the way for innovative teaching and learning. To my challenging, persistent, intellectually demanding students at the Intensive English Institute, thank you for pushing me to justify my pedagogy; to you I am indebted. Finally, thank you to my ever-supportive husband David, and to my daughter Elisheva, for their encouragement and belief that hours of Mum sat tapping at the keyboard would result in something good!

ABOUT THE AUTHOR

Aviva Katzenell is the Academic Director of the Intensive English Institute (IEI) at Florida Atlantic University. She has taught English in different capacities for over 20 years in the United Kingdom, Middle East, and the United States, and her education includes an MA TESOL, MPhil Publishing Studies, PGCE in English, and a BA (hons) in English Literature and Linguistics. She is a seasoned teacher-trainer, presenter, and curriculum designer and loves her professional role as it includes teaching and learning, student and faculty engagement, innovative pedagogy, and being part of a thriving community which serves English language learners from all over the world. Her vision for the IEI supports a rigorous classroom curriculum together with language learning through extracurricular activities. First and foremost, Aviva is a voracious reader and lover of language.

CONTENTS

FIGURES AND TABLES

FIGURES:

TABLES:

ACRONYMS AND ABBREVIATIONS

CEFR: Common European Framework of Reference for Languages
EAP: English for academic purposes.
ESL: English as a second language.
ESP: English for specific purposes.
IEP: Intensive English program.
SLOs: Student learning outcomes.
TESOL: Teachers of English to Speakers of Other Languages

FOREWORD: THEORY AND PRACTICE, BITE-SIZED ACTIVITIES FOR TEACHING READING SKILLS

A personal note:

At the age of 10, I was uprooted from my hometown of Glasgow, Scotland, and whisked away to Israel. Up until that point, I was top of my class with a reading age beyond my years; I was 'that' kid marched to the reading cupboard several grades up, and the kid who read voraciously by torchlight under the covers at night. I was considered bright and able by parents and teachers, and a bespectacled nerd by my peers. Unfortunately, despite being taught basic reading and writing in Hebrew at school, I was not prepared for reading—or learning—in another language. I was plonked down in a fifth grade Israeli classroom and expected to soak up math, history, social sciences, and biology in a second language (L2). My ability to read the four questions in Hebrew on Passover, or say the basic prayers on Saturday at Temple were scant preparation for the huge cognitive burden that awaited me in an L2 classroom.

I couldn't read Hebrew in volume. Or I could, but didn't want to: it was *too* darned hard. I did, however, continue reading in English: Jane Austen, Dickens, Terry Pratchett, all the classics, every crime novel, and every thriller I could get my hands on. My English, now self-taught, flourished; my reading in Hebrew, on the other hand, not so much. Surprisingly, my spoken Hebrew was more than adequate; Broca's area had not yet lost its plasticity, and the sounds and tones of Hebrew posed no problem phonologically. However, the sheer burden of decoding the written word, letter-by-letter, word-by-word, sentence by sentence proved too much for me. My eyes were used to flying over pages in English at breakneck speed—why couldn't I replicate this in an L2?

In addition to the cognitive burden of tracking, decoding, and putting letters and words together, there was another substantial difficulty—many of the cultural, historical, and contemporary references were lost to me. Language does not denote only the physical and concrete; language is a channel for the abstract, the conceptual, the sounds, smells, touch, and taste of an unfamiliar landscape, history, and presence. Avoid reading, and lose vocabulary, sentence structure, grammar, and most importantly, belonging.

Fast forward 40-plus years to Boca Raton, Florida Atlantic University, and so many of my students study English in order to integrate into academic institutions, professional jobs, or just to survive in the United States. Without the ability to read intensively, strategically, and extensively, they cannot do so. With a heavy cognitive burden, and elusive cultural references, my students do not and cannot fully integrate. This is why this guide is so important. With a focus on strategies for reducing the cognitive burden and on strategies for providing access to cultural references, teachers may just open pathways to their students' dreams, or at the very least, lighten a very difficult load.

Introduction

Welcome to *Theory and Practice: Bite-sized Activities for Teaching Reading Skills*. This is *not* an arduous trek up the mountain of research provided by giants such as Naomi Baron, William Grabe, Keith Stanovich, Maryanne Wolf, and so many others; instead, it is a gentle stroll along a clearly marked pathway lined with useful reading skills activities, and supported by just enough theory to justify *what* we teach, *how* we teach, and *why* we teach reading skills. Our bright, intelligent students aim to reach that English language learning mountain peak, and do so motivated by logical, sensible explanations for activities and tasks; and even though we thrive on teaching intuitively and organically, we need to ask how many of us do so mindfully, intentionally supported by theory-based knowledge. This volume, therefore, is not an insurmountable mountain of research and activities, but an informative, practical stroll along a gentle incline, wind in our hair, sun at our back, and reading skills an achievable and enjoyable journey.

What Will this Book Help the Teacher Do?

This volume will provide instructors of intensive English programs, community and adult English as a second language (ESL) courses, and private ESL teachers with approaches to teaching reading skills, together with activities suitable for high-beginner levels to low-advanced students. This guide is especially useful for student teachers looking for an accessible, explanatory framework for reading skills theory and practice, and for practicing teachers looking for inspiration at any given time in the teaching cycle. Chapter 1 provides teachers with theory on word recognition, phonemic awareness, reading comprehension, discourse structure, and extensive reading. Chapters 2 to 4 focus on practical activities that lend themselves to academic, professional, and personal English language learning goals and can be adapted to different levels, different age groups, and online platforms. Chapter 5 provides a brief guide to adapting all the activities in chapters 2 to 4 online. Readers will also encounter references to and explanations of Color Vowel® throughout this book: a brain-based methodology for building phonemic awareness, Color Vowel® is a powerful tool for enhancing productive skills such as speaking and writing *and* receptive skills such as listening and reading.

As you embark on this reading skills journey, please keep in mind that the reading process is truly a miracle: the brain was never wired for reading! While the brain excelled at visual and aural perception honed for survival since the dawn of humanity, the creation of new neural pathways to visually identify symbols on clay, papyrus, and print and then link these representations to the sounds of spoken language is a fairly new endeavor, a mere six thousand years old. Originating in Ancient Sumer, otherwise known as Mesopotamia, or modern-day Iraq, visual symbols as representations of information, ideas, and abstract concepts developed as the result of trade, economics, and war. Astonishingly for the effortless reader, our brains created new connections amid older neural pathways and created links to what we *see*, to what we *hear*, and finally to what we already *know*. With its natural plasticity and 'open architecture' (Wolf, 2008), our brains fired up new structures to specialize linking sounds to symbols and to our own mental landscapes and experiences. *What* we read, *why* we read, and *how* we read in the educational frameworks of our intensive English programs (IEPs), community ESL courses, small groups, and one-to-one English classes are questions we will explore in the coming chapters.

I hope you will enjoy this book; it is the volume I wish I'd had before waltzing haplessly into the classroom so many years ago.

Pedagogy Behind the Practice

The English teaching market is awash with teaching materials in print and online. Punch in intermediate reading activities for adults, English for academic purposes (EAP), K-12, or any other level or category of student, and a plethora of websites offer reading texts, activities, and exercises. The question remains, though: how much of our classroom teaching is pedagogically driven? Do we know *why* a particular activity is useful? I'd like to say yes, but I suspect, from experience, this is not always the case. While vocabulary lists or cloze exercises look promising, are they structured and scaffolded to lower the learning burden, or are they a nice ten-minute filler with no real learning outcome in mind? As professionals, we aim to be effective; we aim to teach purposefully and intentionally; and when our students make significant progress due to carefully scaffolded, structured learning with clear goals, objectives and student learning outcomes, we bask in their joy and teach with a renewed spring in our step and twinkle in our eyes.

To assist in mindful and purposeful teaching and learning, this volume aims to introduce key elements of reading pedagogy. We will consider the brain and its function in recognizing symbols on the page and discuss the physiological process of reading: how our eyes track symbols on the page and why we should consider this process before confronting our students with large volumes of text. We will consider the connection between sound and reading: why phonemic awareness is *so* important to reading skills and how we map sounds to letters when English orthography, or spelling, is deep and irregular. We will delve briefly into sound awareness as part of our pre-reading activities, examine Color Vowel® methodology as a useful tool for linking sound to written symbol, and discuss *schema theory*, the value of activating students' prior knowledge and experience, or as Gibbons (2015) states, their "in-the-head knowledge" *before* our students read and discover why utilizing students' pre-existing knowledge is crucial for introducing new vocabulary, text, and mental landscapes.

We will also consider the importance of *top-down processing* and *bottom-up processing*. Do students absorb abstract ideas and concepts first, or do they invest time and effort in reading each letter, word, phrase, and sentence? Do these processes occur simultaneously, and what does this mean for how we teach strategic reading? We will discuss when and how top-down processing and bottom-up processing occur, and the importance of *automaticity* (Grabe and Yamashita 2022), the ability to retrieve vocabulary and syntactic knowledge quickly from *long-term memory*. Moreover, since our students are active participants in the act of reading, not empty vessels or passive recipients of information, we will discuss the reading strategies, or *scaffolding*, that enable our students to take that interactive leap and employ *working memory* capacity for critical thinking skills.

Finally, we'll examine *extensive reading* and its pedagogical value within tight teaching schedules, and the value of post-reading activities for summary, paraphrase, and consolidation of vocabulary, syntax, and critical thinking skills. Since we have established the brain is fairly new to reading, and since we are moving from an age of literacy to the digital age, we will also consider the media used for reading skills, print versus digital, and whether this affects how our students physically read, think, and retain information. With an understanding of the physiological process of reading, the crucial aspects of pre-reading activities, the need for strategic and interactive reading, and the consolidation of reading through post-reading activities, we can march proudly into that classroom, present our students with thoughtful, intentional activities, and pat ourselves firmly on the back: we know *what* we are doing, *how* we are doing it, and perhaps, most importantly, *why*!

Chapter 1

Competencies and Standard-Based Frameworks for Teaching Reading Skills: What Do We Teach and Why?

Curriculum is at the heart of every English language course. Based on needs analysis—what our students need to learn and why—we identify our curricular goals, create the objectives, the way we are going to cover those goals, and finally, the student learning outcomes (SLOs). These lofty plans determine both our overall curriculum and our long-term, medium-term, and short-term lesson plans. But how do we know what reading skills our students require; and how can we tell where they are in an overall reading skills journey?

Additionally, if you've ever begun a new teaching job only to be told you are the lucky recipient of Level 3, did you panic (like me) and wonder what Level 3 actually referred to? Is this a pre-intermediate class? Intermediate? Something else? Like me, were you too embarrassed to ask for clarification thinking you'd figure it out once you entered the classroom? And did your syllabus clearly identify goals, objectives, and SLOs? Who planned your curriculum? Was it you, or was it handed down from above with the expectation that you decode another instructor's thought process? If your answer is yes or I'm not quite sure to any of the above, access to clearly defined English language teaching standards would have been extremely handy.

There are several such standards-based frameworks available to teachers based on geographical location, needs analysis of the population, and links to relevant assessment. The Common European Framework of Reference for Languages (CEFR), the Global Scale of English (GSE), and the Comprehensive Adult Student Assessment System (CASAS) all provide standards with measurable competencies. Additional assessment tools such as the International Language Testing System (IELTS), Test of English as a Foreign Language (TOEFL), and the Duolingo English test are accepted by educational institutions across the globe as accurate indicators of English competencies. Also, the TESOL International Association, the largest professional organization for teachers of English as a second or foreign language, provides guidance in the form of *6 Principles for Exemplary Teaching of English Learners* (Short et al, 2018) that offer insight and particulars on essential elements for successful English language teaching and learning. Based on whether students require English for academic, professional, or personal reasons, whether students require common core English (elementary through secondary school), EAP, or ESP, institutions will choose their curricular framework and determine which one serves their students' needs best.

The CEFR Framework

The CEFR is my chosen framework. Aligned with most well-known academic and general TESOL publishers, it provides internationally recognized level descriptors for core English and enables us to determine, not only what we mean by high-beginner to high-advanced learners, but also provides us with general and detailed descriptors for each category. It does so not only for English, but for a wide array of languages, making sure level descriptors paint an accurate picture of language learners' journey from basic user to proficient user in a standardized, international, accountable framework: "It describes in a comprehensive way what language learners . . . learn to do in order to use a language for communication and what knowledge and skills they have to develop so as to be able to act effectively" (Council of Europe, 2020).

As a useful starting point for the uninitiated, the CEFR divides language learners into three separate categories: basic users, independent users, and proficient users. These categories in turn are divided into the following levels:

- basic users: A1 high beginners; A2 pre-intermediate learners.
- independent users: B1 intermediate learners; B2 upper-intermediate learners.
- proficient users: C1 low-advanced learners; C2 high-advanced learners ready for direct admission to university with near-native language proficiency.

The CEFR then lists each level and explains its overall goals in both general templates and more specific details. Since we are trying to lower the learning burden not only for students, but also ourselves within a busy teaching schedule, CEFR's *Common Reference Levels: Global Scale* (Table 1.1), makes an excellent framework for our overall curriculum, and provides us

Table 1.1 Common Reference Levels: Global Scale

PROFICIENT USER	C2	Can understand with ease virtually everything heard or read. Can summarize information from different spoken and written sources. reconstructing arguments and accounts in a coherent presentation. Can express him/herself spontaneously. very fluently and precisely. differentiating finer shades of meaning even in more complex situations.
	C1	Can understand a wide range of demanding longer texts. and recognize implicit meaning. Can express him/herself fluently and spontaneously without much obvious searching for expressions. Can use language flexibly and effectively for social, Academic, and professional purposes. Can produce clear, well-structured, detailed text on complex subjects. showing controlled use of organizational patterns, connectors, and cohesive devices.
INDEPENDENT USER	B2	Can understand the main ideas of complex text on both concrete and abstract topics, including technical discussions in his/her field of specialization. Can interact with a degree of fluency and spontaneity that makes regular interaction with native speakers quite possible without strain for either party. Can produce clear, detailed text on a wide range of subjects and explain a viewpoint on a topical issue giving the advantages and disadvantages of various options.
	B1	Can understand the main points of clear standard input on familiar matters regularly encountered in work, school, leisure, etc. Can deal with most situations likely to arise whilst travelling in an area where the language is spoken. Can produce simple connected text on topics which are familiar or of personal interest. Can describe experiences and events. dreams, hopes & ambitions, and briefly give reasons and explanations for opinions and plans.

(Continued)

Table 1.1 *Continued*

BASIC USER	A2	Can understand sentences and frequently used expressions related to areas of most immediate relevance (e.g., very basic personal and family information, shopping, local geography, employment). Can communicate in simple and routine tasks requiring a simple and direct exchange of information on familiar and routine matters. Can describe in simple terms aspects of his/her background, immediate environment, and matters in areas of immediate need.
	A1	Can understand and use familiar everyday expressions and very basic phrases aimed at the satisfaction of needs of a concrete type. Can introduce him/herself and others and can ask and answer questions about personal details such as where he/she lives, people he/she knows, and things he/she has. Can interact in a simple way provided the other person talks slowly and clearly and is prepared to help.

Source: Council of Europe (2020).

with a common language when discussing identifying features for each level. (Council of Europe, 2020).

Table 1.1 indicates the following:

- At the A1 or high-beginner level, both receptive (listening and reading) and productive (speaking and writing) skills are very basic and focus on phrases linked to introduction, simple questions, and personal details.
- At the A2 or pre-intermediate level, students' receptive and productive skills engage with immediate, personal needs: family, shopping, the local environment.
- At the B1 or intermediate level, students are able to understand text regarding school, family, leisure, employment, and should be able to identify both main ideas and details in these texts. They should be able to produce simple connected text and describe hopes, wishes, and provide reasons.
- At the B2 or upper-intermediate level, students require automaticity: storage of language in long-term memory, ability to

identify key ideas, report on details, engage with technical as well as general text, and produce clear and detailed writing.

- At the C1 or low-advanced level, students require inference skills, automaticity, the ability to synthesize texts while appraising them critically, and the ability to produce well-structured, cohesive and coherent sophisticated writing.
- At the C2 or high-advanced level, students have near native language skills.

It is important to note that the CEFR covers core English, or general English. Tertiary institutions with a focus on EAP will interpret levels B1 to C1 with academic language and text.

In terms of reading skills, CEFR's overall reading comprehension table (Table 1.2) identifies stages in the reading comprehension journey and

Table 1.2 Common Reference Levels: Overall Reading Comprehension

C2	*Can understand and interpret critically virtually all forms of the written language including abstract, structurally complex, or highly colloquial literary and non-literary writings.*
	Can understand a wide range of long and complex texts, appreciating subtle distinctions of style and implicit as well as explicit meaning.
C1	*Can understand in detail lengthy, complex texts, whether or not they relate to his/her own area of speciality, provided he/she can reread difficult sections.*
B2	*Can read with a large degree of independence, adapting style and speed of reading to different texts and purposes, and using appropriate reference sources selectively. Has a broad active reading vocabulary, but may experience some difficulty, with low-frequency idioms.*
B1	*Can read straightforward factual texts on subjects related to his/her field and interest with a satisfactory level of comprehension.*
A2	*Can understand short, simple texts on familiar matters of a concrete type which consist of high-frequency everyday or job-related language.*
	Can understand short, simple texts containing the highest frequency vocabulary, including a proportion of shared international vocabulary items.
A1	*Can understand very short, simple texts a single phrase at a time, picking up familiar names, words, and basic phrases and rereading as required.*

Source: Council of Europe (2020).

provides descriptors for each level. This information is general, but provides clear orientation points for both curriculum designers and language learners along the language learning journey.

Table 1.2 indicates the following:

- At the A1 or high-beginner level, the focus is on very short texts, rereading, and building familiarity with basic vocabulary, simple words and phrases.
- At the A2 or pre-intermediate level, the focus is on short, simple texts, high-frequency language related to everyday jobs, school, and leisure-related language.
- At the B1 or intermediate level, there is a move towards more independent comprehension of factual texts related to common interests.
- At the B2 or upper-intermediate level, students comprehend a wider range of texts with little difficulty, with the exception of low-frequency expressions.
- At the C1 or low-advanced level, students read a wide array of complex texts and grapple with sophisticated language outside their scope of interest.
- At the C2 or high-advanced level, students read virtually all text, are aware of nuance, subtleties, explicit and implicit meaning.

Different student populations have different goals and, therefore, different student outcomes: students in elementary, secondary, and tertiary institutions have academic focuses to contend with; adult English classes in community ESL programs may focus on survival English; multilingual domestic students may wish to improve their general English skills. However, with the CEFR distinctions above as a general framework for reading competencies, student learning outcomes might look like the following:

A1: high-beginner reading SLOs

- ☐ Identify main idea of short passages at the high-beginner level
- ☐ Infer basic vocabulary from context
- ☐ Interpret simple charts, maps, and forms

A2: pre-intermediate reading SLOs

- ☐ Identify main ideas and supporting details in a simple reading text on social, professional, and pre-academic themes
- ☐ Restate main ideas of different reading passages verbally and in writing
- ☐ Infer meaning from text and determine meaning from context and cues in reading texts

B1: intermediate reading SLOs

- ☐ Distinguish between main ideas and supporting details, infer meanings and opinions in readings, use context cues to determine meaning of unfamiliar words and phrases
- ☐ Identify central theme in multi-paragraph general English and pre-academic readings
- ☐ Identify high-frequency academic verb forms and vocabulary for expressing opinion, consequence, sequence, addition, and argument

B2: upper-intermediate reading SLOs

- ☐ Distinguish between main ideas and supporting details in academic texts and general readings
- ☐ Demonstrate reading strategies such as previewing, skimming, and scanning
- ☐ Demonstrate reading strategies such as identifying pronoun referents, summarizing, and inferring from context
- ☐ Identify central theme in multi-paragraph academic readings
- ☐ Use context cues to determine meaning of unfamiliar words and phrases
- ☐ Infer meaning, mood, bias, and tone in increasingly complex readings

C1: low-advanced

- ☐ Distinguish between main ideas, details, and examples in a wide array of academic texts and general readings
- ☐ Identify central argument in research articles
- ☐ Infer meaning, mood, bias, and tone in readings
- ☐ Utilize context cues to determine the meaning of unfamiliar words and phrases
- ☐ Summarize and paraphrase sourced material

C2 learners are advanced with near-native English language competencies and do not require English language teaching at elementary, secondary, or tertiary levels.

As an instructor and curriculum designer, I have found CEFR extremely useful for highlighting learner competencies at different levels. Furthermore, if you look carefully at leading English language teaching textbooks, you will generally find reference to CEFR levels on back covers and within their catalogs. You will also find relevant reading skills along with SLOs at the beginning of each unit and can tell at a glance whether your chosen materials are suitable for your students at their particular journey point. This creates an alignment of goals, objectives, and student learning outcomes: CEFR provides internationally recognized language learning standards; CEFR-aligned textbooks provide materials and exercises that meet these standards; and our curriculum-designed SLOs indicate our student outcomes at the end of each level. Even if teachers' or institutions' chosen frameworks differ from the CEFR, understanding the nomenclature provides us with a clearer understanding of learning levels and the competencies involved.

Most importantly, when faced with a "Level 3," we now have objective language to describe the student at this level. Asking our supervisor if Level 3 is A2, pre-intermediate, immediately clarifies their level within an overall program structure and determines the goals, objectives, and student learning outcomes for the level; it also shows we are professionals aware of international English language learning standards. If only I'd been more aware of the CEFR, or similar frameworks, at the beginning of my own teaching journey, I might have entered the classroom more intentionally, more aware, and definitely better prepared!

The Reading Process

As skilled readers, English instructors might not consciously engage with the physiological or cognitive reading process. Reading, as we've mentioned, is not an innate human skill; our ability to decode graphic symbols and construct meaning are learnt skills and involve different mechanisms: visually, light hits the retina of the eye and cells called photoreceptors turn the light into electrical signals that travel from the retina, through the optic nerve to the brain, which turns the signals into images (Moats and Tolman, 2004; Grabe, 2014). We visually register these images or graphemes on the page, and with our eyes, move forward in a rapid series of saccades—otherwise known as jumps—and fixations. Each "fixation," or visual focus of approximately 0.25 milliseconds for the L1 reader, views content words: nouns, verbs, adjectives, and adverbs. The brain, though, processes each letter individually, taking in a span of seven to nine letters to the right, and three to four letters to the left: how else would we read *cause* instead of *clause*, or *photograph* instead of *phonograph*? The expert reader zooms through text pausing only to grapple with difficult concepts or enjoy a particularly well-turned phrase. If fluent L1 readers cover between 240 to 300 words per minute (depending on context and reading purpose), L2 students in a secondary and university context typically cover 70 to 100 words per minute (Grabe and Yamashita, 2022) and do so with slower reading rates and fixation times (Nisbet et al., 2021). L2 learners, therefore, not only grapple with definition, syntax, and unfamiliar cultural references, but physically engage in a longer, more strenuous struggle each time they put eyes and brain to digital print or paper.

The reader with automaticity—excellent word recognition skills and morphological and syntactic knowledge—will "jump" forward with more capacity for engaging working memory in comprehension and analysis (Park, 2018); the reader unfamiliar with vocabulary, and unable to situate its function within a phrase, clause, or sentence, will jump backwards, or "regress," and use more working memory for word recognition and less for critical thinking. Regressions might be short and focus on a few letters within a word, or they might be longer and include earlier words in a sentence, or even previous sentences within a text; the former suggests specific word processing difficulties; the latter comprehension failures of entire sentences within a larger text (Roberts and Siyanova-Chanturia, 2021). *We* might fly through a general English text with ease, but our students use an enormous amount of energy as they focus on text with unfamiliar words, complex syntax, and abstract concepts. Through teaching reading skills discretely, we aim to develop automaticity and move from regressions to immediate access to the mental lexicon and development of higher-order reading skills such as reading for critical thinking and reading to learn.

Phonemic Awareness and Fluency

Grabe and Yamashita (2022) cover six models of reading comprehension: the Simple View of Reading, Construction–Integration model, Landscape View of Reading, Verbal Efficiency model, and a reading systems framework approach;

they favor the latter as it suggests reading develops from a wide range of reading experiences and the use of underlying cognitive skills. However, all models include one essential component: the connection between phonemic awareness and reading. In order to read, the brain must register sound and match phoneme (sound) to grapheme (symbol); this in turn creates a mental concept which leads to comprehension and interpretation of the written word. L1 readers in childhood learn to decode graphemes and link visuals on the page to phonemes and to sounds. Gibbons (2015) reminds us the ability to distinguish between the distinctive sounds of the language and learn how the sounds are represented in print, constitutes a crucial foundation for decoding words and developing knowledge of the alphabetic system. Stanovich (2009) asserts that children who "crack" the spelling-to-sound code early on are forecast to display superior academic achievement, and Wolf (2008) talks at length about children who cannot map sounds to letters and the difficulties they encounter. Finally Grabe and Yamshita (2022) reference Baddley (2007) and state that "storage, rehearsal, and reinforced memory of words in phonological form are the foundation of all vocabulary learning, and much of language learning in general." In short, the ability to read c-a-t and link each individual grapheme to a known sound and blend both sounds and letters to form a mental representation of the word is essential for decoding the written word, accessing meaning, and developing a large mental lexicon with extensive vocabulary.

But, wait, I hear you say! We teach L2s at EAPs or community ESL courses; we teach adults, not children, and they already have neural pathways for decoding symbols in their own languages. Indeed, Chinese children develop brain architecture to decode 2000 logograms by the age of seven (Wolf, 2008); Hebrew speakers develop the ability to read words comprised of consonants without the need for diacritics or written vowels (Frost in Snowling and Hulme 2005); surely the link between sound and letter is only a hop, skip, and a saccade away. Actually, no. Not only do Miriam Burt et al. (2017) remind us that adult English language learners whose L1 is written with the Roman alphabet still have difficulty with phonological processing, but after puberty, Broca's area, the brain region concerned with speech production, loses plasticity and L2s struggle to hear the sounds and intonations of English, especially if their L1 is very different (Taylor, 2020). This explains why Asian students find it difficult to pronounce end consonants, why Arabic speakers glottalize and sound choppy in English, and why Spanish speakers struggle with the difference between /sheet/ and /sh*t /, /beach/ and /b*tch/. If they cannot *hear* these sounds, internalize them, and consciously map these phonemes (sounds) onto corresponding graphemes (symbols), consider how difficult the reading process and reading comprehension becomes!

Furthermore, when it comes to spelling, English has *deep orthography* (Frost, cited in Snowling and Hulme (2005). In Spanish, there is phoneme-to-grapheme correspondence; theirs is a *shallow* orthography: *la ortografía española es fácil* sounds like it reads. English orthography, however, is deep and makes little sense to the novice or developing reader: *English spelling is easy*? The "E" of /English/ sounds like the "i" in /igloo/; the "ee" sound in /easy/ is spelt "ea," and the "s" sound in /easy/ sounds like a "z." What's an L2 learner to do? Illustrating this point just a little further is the well-known poem *The Chaos* by Gerard Nolst Trenité (n.d.) with *800* irregularities of pronunciation and spelling.

The poem begins like so:

> Dearest creature in creation
> Studying English pronunciation,
> I will teach you in my verse
> Sounds like corpse, corps, horse and worse.
> I will keep you, Susy, busy,
> Make your head with heat grow dizzy;
> Tear in eye, your dress you'll tear;
> Queer, fair seer, hear my prayer.
> Pray, console your loving poet,
> Make my coat look new, dear, sew it!
> Just compare heart, hear and heard,
> Dies and diet, lord and word.

It includes both visually and phonemically painful verses such as:

> Now I surely will not plague you
> With such words as vague and ague,
> But be careful how you speak,
> Say: gush, bush, steak, streak, break, bleak,
> Billet does not end like ballet;
> Bouquet, wallet, mallet, chalet.
> Blood and flood are not like food,
> Nor is mould like should and would.

And it ends with:

> Don't you think so, reader, *rather*,
> Saying *lather, bather, father*?
> Finally, which rhymes with *enough*,
> *Though, through, bough, cough, hough, sough, tough*??
> *Hiccough* has the sound of *sup* . . .
> My advice is: GIVE IT UP!
>
> (Published in The New River Project, 1995)

We do *not* want our students to "GIVE IT UP!" We want our students to read easily, fluently, and with comprehension. But consider, once again, the huge cognitive burden we place on our students as we ask them to read in English. As Trenité's poem demonstrates, English vowel sounds in particular confound all sense of logic and place obstacles at word recognition level. We ask our learners to detour from neural pathways created specifically for the sounds and symbols of native mother tongues, create new ones to accommodate English sound and symbols, and carry an increasingly heavy backpack of new vocabulary, morphology, syntax, content, and critical thinking skills to boot. What began as an exciting hike up reading skills mountain has turned into an exhausting excursion with little end in sight.

Furthermore, word acquisition is only a partial ingredient of reading fluency.

> Fluency is the ability to read rapidly with ease and accuracy and to read with appropriate prosodic words stress and phrasing while understanding the text . . . it is what allows readers to process much larger amounts of input, expand the breadth and depth of their vocabulary . . . increase content knowledge, develop automatic word recognition skills, read for additional learning and build reading motivation.
>
> (Grabe and Yamashita, 2022)

Whether reading out loud or silently, recognition of thought groups, rising and falling intonation, and stress lead to fluency, both the "antecedent and consequence of comprehension" (Sweet and Snow, 2003 cited in Grabe and Yamashita 2022). Our students require phonemic awareness for both oral reading *and* silent reading if they are to read fluently, automatically, and with comprehension.

Many IEPs, masters in TESOL courses and TESOL publications use the international phonetic alphabet (IPA), to link sound to symbol. To me, an alumnus of countless phonetics and linguistics courses, the IPA is still a world of mystery and challenge. In order to teach one language, students—and instructors—must first master another: the vowel sound /a/ in /cat/ looks like **/æ/**; the /e/ sound in /bed/ looks like **/ɛ/;** moving vowels such as /ow/ in /brown cow/ looks like **/aʊ/**. Consonants such as /th/ in /this/ appear as **/θ/** while /th/ in /this/ or /that/ appear as **/ð/**. For those linguistically minded, the IPA chart and symbols is a wonder to behold; for the L2 learner, it is yet another unnecessary burden to overcome. Furthermore, pronunciation manuals discuss short and long vowels: the **/æ/** in /mat/ and the **/ɛ/** in bed are considered short, while the **/e^y/** in /mate/ or the **/i^y /** in /bead/ are considered long. However, as Taylor (2020) points out, the **/æ/** sound in /mat/ can be held for as many seconds as one can hold one's breath. Similarly, the **/e^y/** sound in /mate/ can be uttered quickly. The terminology, the symbols, and time limitations leave students—and teachers—with a heavy cognitive burden.

Fortunately, Taylor et al. (2016) have found magnificent ways to overcome phoneme-grapheme correspondence difficulties. They encourage activation of other brain areas to compensate for Broca's area and do so via the use of visuals, music of rhythm and chant, knowledge of primary stress, and kinesthetic movement. Crucially, they link sound to color instead of linking sound to spelling. /Women/ may include the letter "o," but the sound pronounced is **/ɪ/**; the words /many/, /best/, /friends/, and /meant/ may contain an **/ɛ/** sound, but the spelling patterns are completely different. Across the world, English for speakers of other languages (ESOL) instructors use Color Vowel® methodology to differentiate /pepper/ from /paper/, and /get/ from /gate/ (see Figures 1.1 to 1.3). As students encounter new vocabulary, they identify the primary stress of each word, its color, and organize newly acquired words and phrases in their Color Vowel® Organizer.

Taylor and Thompson suggest introducing new vocabulary in the following manner:

1. *Say* the word with arm extended to signify length on peak vowel (the stressed vowel), and open the hand to indicate primary stress.
2. *Look* at the word in written form, identify its corresponding color, and underline the primary stress.
3. *Record* the word with its primary stress and corresponding color in the Color Vowel® Organizer.

How exciting is it to log the words /any/, /best/, friend/, /meant/ under the color RED PEPPER. What happens when students encounter the words /many/ and /leant/ in their reading texts? Since they have previously encountered and recorded /any/ and /meant/, will they already have a mental pattern

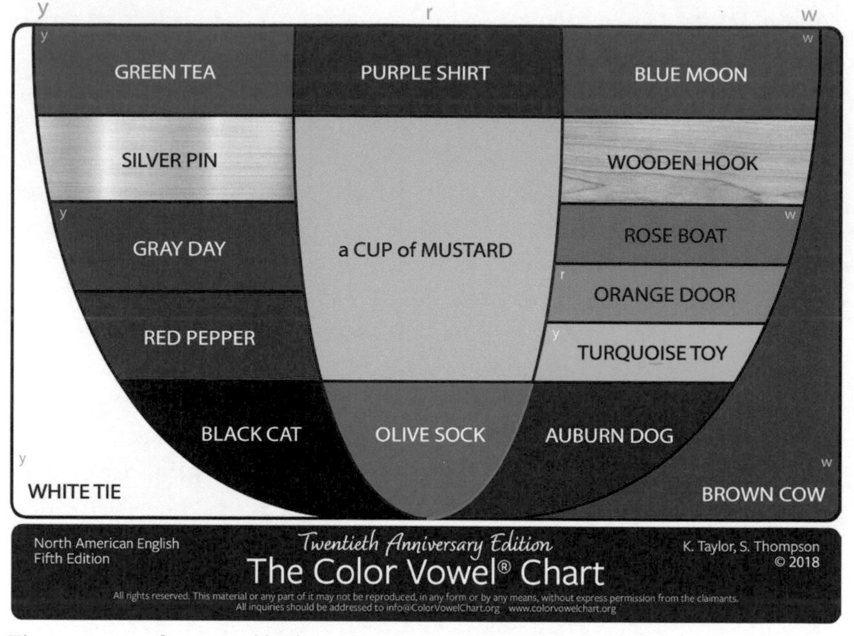

Figure 1.1 Color Vowel® Chart (Taylor and Thompson, 2018)

- GREEN TEA teacher
- SILVER PIN women
- GRAY DAY paper
- RED PEPPER bed
- BLACK CAT hat
- OLIVE SOCK stop
- AUBURN DOG blog
- TURQUOISE TOY enjoy
- ORANGE DOOR source
- ROSE BOAT go
- WOODEN HOOK book
- BLUE MOON two
- A CUP OF MUSTARD one
- PURPLE SHIRT skirt
- BROWN COW wow
- WHITE TIE sky

Figure 1.2 Anchor phrases and example corresponding vocabulary with primary vowel sound and stress underlined.

COLOR VOWEL® Organizer (CVO)

GREEN TEA

WHITE TIE

BLUE MOON
two

SILVER PIN
women

BROWN COW
wow

WOODEN HOOK
women

ROSE BOAT
go

GRAY DAY

PURPLE SHIRT

ORANGE DOOR

RED PEPPER
best friend said
any bread

a CUP of MUSTARD
one

TURQUOISE TOY

BLACK CAT

OLIVE SOCK
stop

AUBURN DOG

Figure 1.3 Color Vowel® Organizer

of sound, color, *and* spelling in their mental lexicon? Will the RED PEPPER sound of /frie̲nd/ remain a spelling anomaly and so stick in the brain as unusual? My own EAP students from A1-C1 view the Color Vowel® as a "hook" to hang their language on. In course evaluations and focus groups throughout the last two years, students have called the Color Vowel® a great equalizer and consistently claim it helps with spelling as they use the Color Vowel® Organizer and log spelling patterns and anomalies. Just as important to me, the instructor, their ability to map sounds to color to spelling patterns supports their reading skills and develops both automaticity and fluency as they progress along their language journey.

Working Memory, Long-Term Memory, and Automaticity in Reading

Laufer and Ravenhorst-Kalovski (2010) suggest that successful reading comprehension relies on a knowledge of 95 to 98 percent of vocabulary in any given text. However, word recognition and acquisition with their phonological components are only *part* of the reading comprehension process. Have you ever asked your students what *they* consider most important to their language learning? I have, and invariably, students will answer "Grammar"; invariably, I will sigh and state that a person desperate for hydration can indicate thirst with one word, "water," no grammar required. Vocabulary is king!

Yulia Ardasheva, winner of the TESOL 2022 Award for Distinguished Research, however highlights the importance of morphological and syntactic knowledge for reading comprehension (2021). Her findings indicate that knowledge of prefixes, suffixes, nouns, verbs, and other speech parts assist L2s in comprehending unfamiliar vocabulary in science, technology, engineering, and mathematics (STEM). While her research has not been replicated in other subject areas, Grabe and Yamashita (2022) support the general idea when asserting that automaticity and fluency occur when readers recognize word forms on the page rapidly, activate phoneme-grapheme correspondence, and then semantic, syntactic, and morphological affixation in more complex words. Nation (2022) states that "knowing" a word involves knowing the members of its word family, its affixes, suffixes, connecting form and meaning, and anything else involving patterns. He further states that storing words in categories and awareness of patterns enables faster access *to* and retrieval *from* the mental lexicon. In other words, in order for *working memory* to work on aspects such as inference, analysis, evaluation, the *long-term memory* stores knowledge of word meaning or representation, its function within clauses, or sentences, and how it relates to words preceding it and words that follow.

For the native English speaker, and certainly for the expert reader, this process takes milliseconds (Wolf, 2008). For the L2 learner, the burden is much greater. In order to truly "know" a word, L2s have to consciously learn morphological forms, collocations, and categories together with associated cultural semantics, referents, and previously unknown mental landscapes. Additionally, Kuhn and Stahl (2003) suggest that "attention expended in one activity is . . . attention unavailable for another." If our students lack automaticity, they expend their efforts on decoding rather than on comprehension and critical thinking skills. For the L2 learner, that gradual incline, or what Nation (2022) terms the "learning burden," has suddenly become quite steep!

Schema Theory

Before we discuss how to ease the cognitive burden involved in reading English, we need to discuss a crucial stage in this language learning journey: *schema theory*. Imagine you are about to embark on your first visit to Mars. You've learnt several Martian symbols and can decode some basic words, letter-by-letter; you are familiar with one or two Martian sounds, and can communicate at A1–Tourist level (a few basic phrases such as "I don't speak Martian"). Your understanding of Martian textual conventions (which do not follow the alphabetic languages' left to right, top to bottom format) is not yet developed, and your experience of Martian textual content, whether basic or academic, is brand new. Beyond that, your mental landscape of Martian culture, habits, food, and architecture is minimal. In short, you do not yet have sufficient prior knowledge, mental structures, *schema* in singular, *schemata* in plural, to relate any text you come across to your own Earth-bound context and experience!

Gibbons (2015) explains schema theory through the lens of reader background and prior knowledge, and states that effective readers draw on personal, culturally acquired knowledge and language to guide and influence the comprehension process. She suggests that readers unable to bring personal knowledge and understanding of a topic to text, are prevented from using a key resource: what they already know! She eloquently states that "meaning does not reside solely in the words of structures of the text but is constructed in the interactions between the text, the in-the-head schematic knowledge of the reader" (140). The reader, it seems, is not a passive receptacle of information, but an interactive participant whose reading of text can only be interpreted in light of the reader's own prior knowledge and experience.

Shuying An (2013) discusses four different types of schemata:

1. Formal schemata relating to the structure and conventions of a text
2. Content schemata related to the content of a text
3. Cultural schemata related to the cultural conventions of a particular population
4. Linguistic schemata relating to linguistic knowledge

For our Arabic students struggling with a left to right Roman alphabet, and for our Chinese students used to logograms, introducing *formal schemata* is essential. For those students unused to reading argument texts and debating the soundness of others' opinions, the structure and discourse conventions of an argument-based text also require *formal schemata*. For those coming from a tropical climate, texts on glaciers require introduction of *content schemata*, and for students new to English, perhaps unaware of Western approaches to evolution, gender, and co-educational learning, *cultural schemata* are essential. Without effective access *to linguistic schemata*, or lexical knowledge, students cannot make sense of formal, content, or cultural schemata.

Where schemata are missing, so are other crucial elements for reading comprehension. *Top-down processing* involves activation of general abstract concepts, and *bottom-up processing* involves knowledge activated by specific data from the text (Grabe and Yamashita 2022). The former is generally viewed as a higher-order skill, and the latter, a lower-order skill. This does not mean, however, that lower-order skills are easier. As readers decode letter-by-letter or gauge a word or phrase's function in a clause or sentence, the brain is working hard! Moreover, while reading, both processes occur simultaneously and confirm predictions, knowledge, patterns, and a sense of where the text is going. If students lack schemata, their path forward is blocked. They cannot relate what they *already know* to key textual concepts while their working memory engages frantically with basic decoding and parsing.

For me, therefore, schemata are crucial to reading success and an essential element of pre-reading tasks. It is an important part of scaffolding for each and every reading lesson; a process of support must be developed within each lesson to create a link between Gibbons' "in-the-head" knowledge of the reader and any new concept constructed within the structure of genre, paragraph, syntax, grammar, and word knowledge. Without activation of what the student already knows, there can be little reading comprehension.

Extensive Reading

Despite the need for explicit teaching of sound, form, and function, Ellis (1996) argues for less explicit attention to formal features, and more to meaning. He sees experience as being an essential component of learning, or implicit learning through continued exposure to the written word. The idea of recycling vocabulary is not new; and the idea that the more students are exposed to text, the more language they encounter, the more they learn seems like common sense. Grabe and Yamashita (2022) advocate recursive teaching of reading skills through reading and rereading of a text. Indeed, much of language learning is recursive; we don't just teach the simple present tense at the A1 level and move on; we engage with the simple present tense, building on its foundation and incrementally adding different tenses all the way to C1. Similarly, we don't abandon simple sentences just because we teach compound and complex sentences; we revisit them throughout each level, reinforcing and analyzing structure and function. The idea of "readers' theatre" in which students read text repeatedly and perform theatrically in order to build automaticity and prosodic awareness, and so engage thoughtfully with meaning, form, content, and prosody, is highly recommended (Young and Nageldinger, 2014). In many English language learning programs, though, time is of the essence. Students are anxious to move up levels; instructors are anxious to cover learning objectives, and it seems that reading comprehension becomes linear instead of recursive: we introduce vocabulary on the environment, read a related text, do some exercises, and in the next lesson move on to a unit on business. Where is the time for revisiting previous vocabulary? Where is the time for theatrical reading? It simply isn't there.

The solution for *extensive reading* is simple: graded readers provide exciting yet accessible texts exposing students to appropriate word families at the appropriate level (Nation and Wang, 2020; Alby, 2017). If students will not/cannot read fiction independently at home, syphon off 30 to 45 minutes a week and read to students in class; expose them to your English language rhythm and tone. Another option is to read an accessible novel for 45 minutes a week. A few examples we've used at the IEI at Florida Atlantic University include: *The Alchemist* by Paulo Coelho at A2 level, *Coraline* by Neil Gaiman at B1 level, Ray Bradbury *Short Stories* at B2 level, and *Of Mice and Men* by John Steinbeck at C1 level. The cultural richness, authentic language evoking plot, character, and tone, and the introduction of schemata referencing students' new encounters with different cultures and landscapes are well worth the 30 to 45-minute deviation from the textbook. As your students revel in their ability to read for pleasure, their linguistic, semantic, and schematic worlds expand.

Reading in the Digital Age

If you can reference 1979 hit song "Video Killed the Radio Star" (Horn et al, 1978), you might not be a digital native and might view ubiquitous technology with suspicion. If that is the case, you are not alone! The fear of new technology supplanting tried and tested methods is as old as the "Radio Star" *and* the fears shared by ancient philosopher Socrates himself! In her book, *Proust and the Squid*, Wolf (2008) describes the horror Socrates felt for the written word and the danger it posed to oral tradition, a form of communication grounded in the search for truth. However, while the idea of recording Homer's tales of godly deeds and kingly quests in writing seemed to diminish the tremendous skills required for oral storytelling, the ability to record those deeds and quests in writing certainly created new pathways in the brain's open architecture (Wolf, 2008). And now that we are moving—or have moved—from the age of literacy to the digital age, we must consider what happens to our students' brains.

Baron (2021) states there is a direct link between perception, motivation, and reading comprehension: students perceive screen reading as easier, and therefore invest less effort, which results in less comprehension. Conversely, she also suggests the ability to read multiple texts on paper—laid out physically and visually more accessible—allows for ease of synthesis and analysis. However, whatever the perception or the reality may be, the phone or laptop screen is now king, libraries are now named media or resource centers, and we must ask the following questions: Does the sheer volume of screen information require different neural pathways? How does scrolling through a phone or reading on a laptop change how we track our letters? Is there even time and room for long-term memory storage or the capacity for inference, analysis, or critique? These are valid questions which English instructors and ELT publishers must address.

The world of publishing reflects the pace of change: major publishers offer their textbooks in digital form. They also offer digital workbooks with consolidation and practice exercises, immediate scoring, percentage of time spent on work, percentage of work completed, and percentage of work submitted correctly. It is an English teacher's dream, not to mention important for the environment. No more hefty textbooks depleting the Amazon rainforest is surely a positive. However, what happens when there is no textbook in class? How do we teach strategic reading skills through annotation? And most importantly, how do we practice communicative skills if our students sit in class with their eyes fixated on their laptops or their phones, instead of the printed page which can be easily annotated, shared, and evaluated with peers?

Baron (2021), Grabe and Yamashita (2022), and Wolf (2008) state there is great danger in this move to digital literacy. The huge amount of information, the rapid scroll-throughs and consequently, the lack of time spent thoughtfully on the written word reveals the reader as a "user of information" rather than an analytical and critical reader. The medium itself makes searching backwards to identify a word, sentence, or idea in the sea of information difficult, and the ability to bookmark a website does not compare to the satisfaction of dogearing a printed page. Wolf especially believes that lacking time to contemplate the written word and shorter, less sophisticated language itself will change the open architecture of the brain, and much like other muscles, the "use it or lose it" notion applies. Most importantly, she sees readers who scroll rapidly through digital pages as impatient, unable to empathize with others, unable to transport themselves to foreign climes or situations, and therefore, unable to walk in others' shoes.

I don't believe video killed the radio star; the video is now obsolete, but I watch my films on Netflix and listen to radio as I drive my car, or late at night to fall asleep. I believe our students require new skills in this digital age and the brain will create new neural pathways to accommodate new types of format. We no longer use clay tablets, papyrus, or parchment, but continue to devour the written word; the phone or screen may supplant paper, but as long as our students require reading skills, we will use the mediums at our disposal.

Wolf (2008), however, makes many salient points. If once upon a time Jane Austin's (1995) opening line to *Pride and Prejudice*—"it is a truth universally acknowledged that a man in possession of a good fortune, must be in want of a wife"—prompted whole monographs, today's response might be "LOL" and a smiley emoji. Unused to grappling with heavy tomes in their own L1, never mind an L2, our students require careful lesson scaffolds whether attempting to access classic literature or social security forms. We cannot allow them to drown in a sea of information and be so overwhelmed by volume that reading is impossible; nor can we allow them to invest less effort in reading online and so miss important information. Additionally, the internet with all its hyperlinks, graphics, distractions, and unverified materials poses yet more barriers to reading comprehension. Students may indeed be "users of information" rather than deep readers, but the cognitive burden involved in decoding the written, printed, or digital word is still very much an issue.

In order to counter this problem, I still require my students to purchase textbooks. I need them to highlight, underline, circle, and write in the margins, and some of the activities in our next chapters require the same. I foresee the day annotation on phones and laptops will be just another tool; until then, I welcome the digital age with all its wondrous applications, but use paper for teaching reading skills if I possibly can. However, if you teach remotely, all the activities in chapters 2 to 4 can be done online. Google's Jamboard allows manipulation of text, notes, and annotation on-screen both individually and collaboratively. Zoom permits sharing materials, annotation, and breakout rooms for small group work, and Webex, Teams, and many other learning platforms such as Canvas and Flipgrid present opportunities for teaching and learning. Additionally, most publishers now produce books in digital form complete with annotation tools. We may not be paperless yet, but digital media afford excellent teaching and learning opportunities with just a little forethought and practice.

Our next chapters aim to support the reading comprehension challenges our students face through adaptable, practical activities and materials. We will activate schema theory, students' prior knowledge and experience, enabling students' interaction with new text, and ensuring their ability to grasp new concepts in light of their own background knowledge. We will use strategic reading to reduce overwhelming text volume and lower cognitive burden, so that engaging with text becomes manageable rather than an ever-retreating horizon. We will log words and phrases in ways to ensure morphological, syntactic, and word-pattern recognition to expand vocabulary and practice automaticity, and we will find ways to link phonemes to graphemes to ensure spelling pattern recognition, and so defeat the puzzles of irregular spelling and sound-to-letter confusion. Finally, we will show our students that reading in an L2 is no barrier to success. The ascent up reading skills mountain may take a while, but it is a journey of joy, replete with knowledge, satisfaction, and achievement. As for you, the instructor, the journey welcomes you as the essential guide.

Chapter 2
Pre-Reading Activities

Now that we've looked at the *what* and the *why*, let's examine the *how*. The activities below provide examples of key reading skills activities; they are easy to implement, tie in directly to theory from chapter 1, and are rewarding for both students and instructor.

Happy teaching!

1. The Thunk

- ✓ Levels A2 to C1
- ✓ Online compatible

> A *Thunk* is a beguilingly simple-looking question about everyday things that stops you in your tracks and helps you start looking at the world in a whole new light . . . At the same time, it encourages you to engage in verbal fisticuffs with the people sitting next to you and, if used properly, always leads to severe brain ache . . .
>
> (Gilbert, 2007)

The mighty **thunk** may appear as a question, statement, and for lower levels, as a visual. Leading ELT textbooks will often provide attractive visuals to act as prompts and questions to elicit personal responses to a topic prior to reading a new text; the materials are excellent, and since they can be expensive, they should be used. Remember, though, the purpose of a *thunk* is intentional.

Link to Theory:

The purpose of a thunk is to:

- activate prior knowledge, experience, and introduce schemata;
- enable the instructor to gauge any gaps in schemata;
- reveal pre-existing knowledge and prior experience of the topic;
- elicit relevant vocabulary, grammar, sentence structure, concepts;

- enable the instructor to gauge any gaps in vocabulary required for text comprehension;
- promote critical thinking skills.

Procedure:

1. Put visuals on whiteboard, or provide visuals for each pair of students.
2. Instruct students to view the visuals and engage in pair discussion.
3. Elicit information from students after paired discussion.
4. Record students' offerings on the board and address any gaps in schemata or vocabulary crucial to new text comprehension.

Example of Thunk Exercise with Visuals:

A1 Topic: Family

Stage 1: Visuals on whiteboard (Figures 2.1 and 2.2).
Stage 2: *Ok, class. What do we see in the pictures? Talk in pairs for three to four minutes.*

Figure 2.1 Mother and Child

Figure 2.2 Father and Child

Stage 3: Elicit information after discussion.

Yes, Mohammad, it looks like the beach. Yes, it's beautiful. Is it morning or night do you think? What else do you see? Ali? A man playing with a child. Holding him up high! Fun! What else? A woman and another child. And a bicycle. Fantastic. Who are the people in the picture? What's that, Svetlana? You think they are a family. You are probably right. Excellent.

What about the second picture? What do we see? A man and a boy. Santiago, you are correct. Father and son? What are they doing? Walking on train tracks. True. Strange. Mohand, do you walk with your son like this? No. Where do you go with your son? To the park. That makes sense. Maria, what about you? Where do you go with your daughter? To the beach . . . like this family? Great.

Stage 4: Record student offerings and address gaps.

So, what are we going to read about in our text today? ***Family****. Great, let's think about vocabulary we can use with family and record it on the board.*

Example of Thunk Exercise with Visuals and Statement:

A2 Topic: Places

A2 reading texts often contain comparisons between urban and rural living since students at this level focus on the personal and familiar: where they live and work. The thunk in the form of visuals *and* statements will elicit students' prior knowledge and experience, relevant vocabulary, grammar, opinions, and, most importantly, personalize the topic pre-reading through tapping into their own mental landscapes and in doing so, enable access to new ones.

Stage 1: Put visuals and statement on the board: ***City life is paradise*** (see Figure 2.3).

Stage 2: *Ok, class: you have 3 to 4 minutes to discuss the statement on the board and look at the picture. What do you think? Agree? Disagree? Is city life "heavenly"? Off you go!*

Stage 3: *Any ideas where this city is? Denis? Yes, New York! How can you tell? Yes, the Statue of Liberty gives it away. Anything else? Tall buildings. Excellent. What about "paradise"? That's an interesting word: yes, Carolina? "The best place." Could be.*

Alejandro? Paradise means heaven for some people. Absolutely! Angels. Are there angels in New York City? Not sure? What's that Maria?

Figure 2.3 New York

Maybe "paradise" means a really good place? Great! So, living in a city is like living in a really good place.

Yousef, what do you think? You agree? Why? Cities are busy and exciting. Excellent vocabulary. What speech parts do we have here? Yes, Carol, adjectives. Very nice.

What about "heavenly"? Luca? That's an adjective too. How can you tell? Great! We add the /l/ and the /y/. Very often adding an /l/ and a /y/ creates an adverb, but in this case, you are correct. It's an adjective. Ok, so Yousef thinks cities are busy and exciting.

Paola, I can see you shaking your head. What do you think? You disagree!Paradise is quiet, no tall buildings with many people, no New York yellow taxis. No river boats with their horns making noise. Ok. You also like green fields, flowers. Where do we find quiet, and green fields? Tatiana? The "country," the "countryside." Excellent.

Stage 4: *How about we create a chart here and compare cities to the countryside? Any suggestions? Let's write them down.*

Thunk activities can be adapted to all levels and all text types. Typical topics in popular ELT textbooks cover subjects such as the environment, globalization, and conservation. Thunks related to these subjects act as models for any topical text. For example:

- B1 topic: The Environment
  thunk: *Recycling is pointless.*
- B2 topic: Globalization
  thunk: *It doesn't matter where my oranges come from as long as they taste sweet!*
- C1 topic: Conservation and Preservation
  thunk: *It is more important to create new objects than to preserve objects from the past.*

2. The Morning Prompt

✓ Levels A2 to C1
✓ Online compatible

The **Morning Prompt** is a truly magnificent tool introduced to the IEI at Florida Atlantic University by colleague Matthew Schaffer. It is an excellent way to encourage reluctant writers to practice timed responses, and reinforces both reading *and* writing skills in a bidirectional manner. Since many writing assignments carry high-stakes grades, this in-class, low-stakes exercise enables students to put pen to paper—or finger to keyboard—to expand the volume of writing over time, incorporate lesson objectives, and reduce fear of writing through consistent timed practice. Most importantly, it enables students to activate prior knowledge and experience before accessing new text.

Link to Theory:

The Morning Prompt acts as a precursor to reading new text and, in doing so, students:

- practice spontaneous, timed writing, and integrate reading and writing skills;
- activate pre-existing knowledge, prior experience, and access schemata;
- activate critical thinking skills;
- practice and consolidate learning presented during the lesson;
- enable the instructor to see if lesson learning objectives have been met and view examples of successful and less successful writing.

Procedure:

1. Provide students with 10 to 15 minutes freewriting in response to a thunk linked to the lesson's new reading text. Instruct students to brainstorm in paragraph form without conscious focus on grammar, vocabulary, or structure; instruct them to pour out their thoughts on the page in response to the prompt.
2. After 10 to 15 minutes freewriting, take whole-class feedback, elicit and record key vocabulary on the board, and any language, grammar, and concepts which may link to the reading text. Elicit and introduce any *missing* key vocabulary, grammar, and concepts necessary for textual comprehension.
3. Read the new text and engage students in textual annotation, exercises, and discussion. You may choose to move to another skill such as grammar or writing post-reading: *any* skill can be incorporated in the final Morning Prompt submission.

4. The following step is crucial: 10 minutes prior to end of lesson, instruct students to edit their initial Morning Prompt response to include an aspect of the lesson's student learning outcomes:
   - If the focus was new vocabulary, instruct them to include 2 to 3 new grammatically correct words in their edited version.
   - If the grammar focus was adjective clauses (as in the following example), instruct them to include 1 or 2 adjective clauses in their response.
   - If the lesson's learning objective was the ability to write comprehensibly about "healthcare models" (as in the following example), ensure editing instructions include reference to the topic.
5. After 10 minutes editing time, instruct students to submit Morning Prompt responses. They can do so on laptops, as hard copies, or upload photographs of their work to the learning platform.
6. Read students' submissions quickly and make a maximum of two to three comments: the point is to provide access to new text through personal response; this is *not* a graded exercise. Instead, award credit for completion!

Example of Morning Prompt:

Students will read a B2 text on "healthcare models" during the lesson. In preparation for reading this text:

Stage 1: Thunk: *Everyone is entitled to free healthcare; a country without free healthcare disregards its people.*
Stage 2: Students write for 10 to 15 minutes and save their response.
Stage 3: Read the new text and continue with the rest of the lesson.
Stage 4: Post-reading/lesson edit instructions:

Morning Prompt: Everyone should be entitled to free healthcare; a country without free healthcare disregards its people. (Figure 2.4.)

- *You have 10 minutes to edit your Morning Prompt.*
- *Include at least one adjective clause with "whose."*
- *Include a minimum of two new vocabulary words/phrases.*

Stage 5: Students submit edited writing.
Stage 6: Instructor reads and comments.

The Morning Prompt works beautifully at levels A2 to C1. Any topic or skill can be the subject of a Morning Prompt and provide access to new text and

Sandra Echererry de Gomez
September 26, 2022
Health is one of the most precious values the the human being have, but it is vulnerable. Because of it in all civilized human system the right to have health care is a basic one. Usually you can find this right written in the constitutions and laws of the democratic countries and even through the practice there are nations whose people have the right and are entitled to a health care a lot of them lack their inclusion inside the system. That is a contradiction because in the paper the right is respected bu in the reality a lot of people lack that kind of support when they have a disease. Thinking about a free health care is beyond the reality in a lot of countries. it requires empathy for its people and a political system that give to them the right to a free health care regardless of their economical status.
Really beautiful, well-expressed writing Sandra! Excellent use of adjective clause with 'whose'. Nice job!
'healthcare' is a non-count noun; do you need an article before it?
New vocabulary word used beautifully in your sentence. Where is a second new word/phrase?

Figure 2.4 Morning Prompt Example

new schema through personal response and activation of prior knowledge and experience. It supports timed response writing and students improve their ability to think, write, and incorporate new ideas the more they practice.

3. The Hot-Seating TV Chat Show

- ✓ Levels A2 to C1
- ✓ Online compatible

The **hot-seating TV chat show** activity provides a wealth of language practice, critical thinking skills, consolidation of prior learning, and prediction skills.

Link to Theory:

Whether reading a novel, a graded reader, or as a precursor to a new text, the hot-seating TV chat show offers students the opportunity to:

- activate schemata;
- practice prediction skills;
- summarize and paraphrase related material;
- ask class members probing questions and practice interrogatives inference, and critical thinking skills;
- describe and analyze character, setting, plot, and language;
- identify thematic patterns, genre language, and conventions;
- experience empathy and have fun in class.

Procedure:

1. Instructor states: *Welcome to the [insert your name here] Chat show!* Show a PowerPoint slide with TV show title, play appropriate music as an opening, and place several chairs in front of the whiteboard area. Hold a fake microphone (I've been known to use a board marker) and welcome the "audience" to a new episode of your daytime TV show. It's noisy, it's fun, and everyone wants to participate.
2. Pick a willing student and bring them to the front as a character from your reading; elicit predictions or summary of knowledge with the student in character. If the student stumbles, elicit the information through questions:
    - Use open questions to elicit thoughtful, more in-depth answers;
    - Use closed questions for specific information.
3. Introduce the next "guests" and invite dialog between them.
4. Invite the audience to ask them questions. It is wonderful running around the classroom, fake microphone in hand, holding it in front of students' mouths as they interrogate fellow classmates as characters in a text or story. Mix it up and investigate motive and nuance: are characters all "good"? Are characters all "bad"? What motives lie behind actions? What can the audience infer about characters, relationships, events?
5. Finally, thank the guests one by one, ask them to leave the stage (go sit down in their seats), and reinforce predictive skills by asking the audience/class what they think will happen next?

Example of Hot-Seating TV Chat Show:

As part of extensive reading, my B1 students read Neil Gaiman's *Coraline*. A particularly spooky novel, it involves a young girl who finds a mirror house within her new home, a "fake" pair of parents intent on sewing buttons on her face for eyes, and a creepy hand that follows her from mirror house to bedroom. This book is not for the faint-hearted, but my class absolutely loved it! In this example, the class has already read chapters 1 and 2 in class and is now preparing for chapter 3.

Stage 1: *Welcome to Aviva's Level 4 TV Chat Show! We have a wonderful show here for you today.*

Stage 2: *A round of applause please for our very special guest, Coraline! Coraline, what's going on at your house?! Can you tell us, what are your parents up to? How do you feel? What have you discovered in the garden, and what does it tell you about your new home?*

Stage 3: *Ladies and gentlemen, let's welcome Coraline's "fake parents" to the show (audience boos); let's also invite Coraline's real parents to the stage and gain their perspective on the family experience.*

Stage 4: *In the novel, Coraline feels abandoned by her real parents; but have they really abandoned her, or are they working hard to provide a roof over Coraline's head and food on the table?* This is the audience's chance to ask insightful, inferential, plot-based, and predictive questions.

Stage 5: *Thank you Coraline, and thank you to both sets of parents, real and fake. And of course, thank you to this wonderful audience. Let's read our* next chapter *and see if your analysis, predictions, and inferences are accurate.*

As students play characters, they recount plot, summarize, analyze character, use topical language, predict next events, and engage in critical thinking skills. All this provides access to the next chapter and consolidates a plethora of learning!

This is an excellent activity for levels A2 to C1, and you can use any text of your choice: graded reader, novel, textbook passage, non-fiction; any text can be turned into a chat show scenario, and any voice turned into role play with your students. Moreover, whether students play a lead character or part of the audience, they are all engaged. A1 students will not yet have sufficient vocabulary to undertake questions and answers; however, the idea can be adapted to a simpler format for this level: teams answering true or false to questions about a reading, character, plot event, or language element; internet or app-based games such as Kahoot! with questions, images, and predictions. Whatever text you use and whatever medium you choose to introduce your characters, students will enjoy the process, consolidate learning, practice reading related skills, and think critically without even realizing they are doing so!

4. The Four-Corner Debate

✓ Levels A1 to C1
✓ Online compatible

The **four-corner debate** is an excellent tool for critical thinking, collaboration, and justification of a position. Before reading a text on food, culture, business, or any other topic, students respond personally to a statement by physically standing in a corner under the headings *Strongly Agree; Agree; Disagree; Strongly Disagree.* In doing so, they activate prior knowledge and experience, express their position, and activate schemata linked to the new text. Even more exciting, after reading the text, students can examine whether their opinions have changed or whether they still belong in the "same corner".

Link to Theory:

The four-corner debate helps to:

- activate prior knowledge, experience, and introduce schemata:
- prompt critical thinking skills;
- introduce relevant vocabulary through group discussion;
- prompt collaboration through communicative activity.

Procedure:

1. Provide a statement thunk on the board relevant to the text you will read in class.
2. Tape a blank poster-sized piece of paper in each corner of the room and add one of the following titles to each one:
   Strongly Agree; Agree; Disagree; Strongly Disagree.

Caveat: students like to 'hedge', so in some cases, the 4-corners debate can become the 2-corners debate to ensure students commit to one position or another.

3. Instruct students to choose their corner—the corner that matches their opinion and enables them to agree, disagree, etc. with the statement on the board—and physically stand there.
4. There are now two options:
   - Collect verbal feedback from each group. Ask students to discuss their position as a group; nominate a group spokesperson or take feedback from willing participants.
   - Ask each group to justify their position by writing the reasons for their stance on the poster paper. Collect feedback from the spokesperson after 10 minutes.
5. As students provide justification, record relevant vocabulary and concepts on the board, elicit further points through questioning, permit students from opposing corners to question each other (politely), and summarize the different positions on the board.
6. Instruct students to sit down then read the new text; the students should now have key vocabulary, phonemic awareness of new vocabulary, and schemata allowing access to the new reading.

Example of Four-Corner Debate Topics:

A2: *It is important to eat American food when you live in America.*
B1: *English language students must only speak English in class.*
B2: *Friends are just as important as family.*
C1: *Exiting your comfort zone is necessary for growth.*

This is a useful tool at the A2 to C1 level for encouraging students to commit to a position. Even students who are hesitant to express themselves out loud can make their way to a corner of the room; it is also physically fun to position oneself bodily in order to represent a stance! Additionally, the collaborative justification of each corner elicits vocabulary, concepts and schemata that will provide a useful pathway into the lesson's new reading material. A change in corner post-reading is an opportunity for evaluative and creative thinking skills and an opportunity to use newly learnt vocabulary and concepts from the new reading text.

This activity works well with A2 to C1 learners, but it can be adapted for A1 learners using clear prompts and two corners: *Agree/Disagree*. For example: *Engineers have the best job.*

Students can position themselves under Agree or Disagree, the instructor can elicit the reasoning behind the positions and record relevant vocabulary on the board.

5. The Diamond Sequence

- ✓ Levels A1 to C1
- ✓ Online compatible

The **diamond sequence** activity was introduced to me during a professional development workshop at King Solomon High School in the United Kingdom many years ago. For all that it's an "oldie," it's a "goodie," and I find myself using different versions of this activity as often as possible. Even students hesitant to express themselves out loud feel comfortable sequencing options, and in doing so activate prior knowledge, experience, and schema before reading a new text.

Link to Theory:

The diamond sequence is an excellent way to:

- pre-teach vocabulary (use images as well as words at the lower levels if necessary);
- focus on speech parts, grammar, pronunciation, and abstract concepts;
- activate prior experience, knowledge, and schemata;
- prompt critical thinking skills;
- encourage collaborative discussion with comparison, contrast, and explanation.

Procedure:

1. Create a set of six to seven "diamonds" with vocabulary, visuals, or statements on their top-facing side.
2. Ask students to sequence their diamond shapes according to *most important* to *least important*. There should be a diamond at the top indicating "most important," a diamond at the bottom indicating "least important," and rows in between where diamonds may carry more or less importance based on student preference. Students can do this individually and then compare, or they can do this in pairs or small groups.
3. Ask students to justify and explain their choices.

Example of Diamond Sequence Exercise:

In preparation for an A1 unit on jobs, students sequence job titles based on their perception of the most important jobs (best) to least important (worst). This is an opportunity to pre-teach relevant vocabulary, encourage collaboration, and support critical thinking skills.

Stage 1: Each student receives a set of diamonds with different jobs and speech parts on top-facing side (Figure 2.5).

Stage 2: *Ok, everyone. Please sequence your diamonds with your best job at the top, your worst at the bottom and the rest in between. Get ready to explain your choices. You have five to seven minutes. Off you go!*

Stage 3: Shihana's sequence (Figure 2.6):

T= Teacher

S = Student Shihana

T: Shihana, your sequence looks really interesting. Can you explain your choices?

S: Businessman at top. Have many businesses. Make a lot of money.

T: True, salary is very important. Computer scientists and engineers also have good salaries. Is that why they are in row 2?

S: Yes.

T: Ok. Shihana, your diamond sequence is very interesting. You have homemaker on the second row. Why?

S: Because is important to cook, and have a good home for family.

T: Ok. It is very important to have a comfortable home. How many people agree with Shihana on that one? Hmn. We'll talk about it a bit later.

What's in your third row? Doctor and artist? Can you explain why?

S: A doctor help people, but work too hard.

T: True, a doctor helps people and works very hard. And the artist?

S: Make life beautiful, but no money.

T: Fair enough. And finally, farmer. Why is farmer at the bottom?

S: Farming very hard. No rain, no grow . . .

T: Crops, no rain means no crops, no wheat or barley or corn. Thank you so much, Shihana.

In the conversation above, Shihana reveals knowledge of vocabulary related to the topic which can then be recorded on the board. She makes an occasional

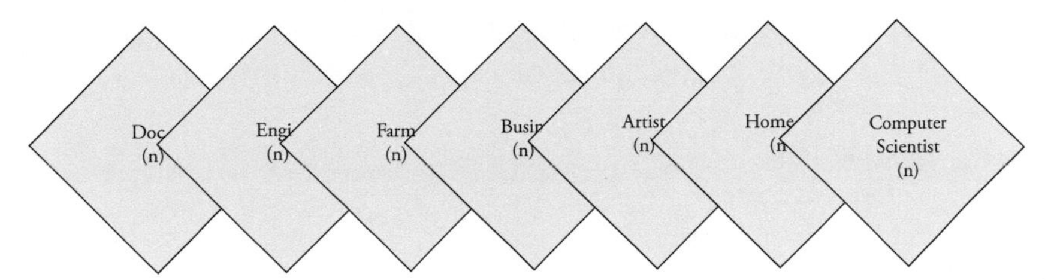

Figure 2.5 Seven Diamonds

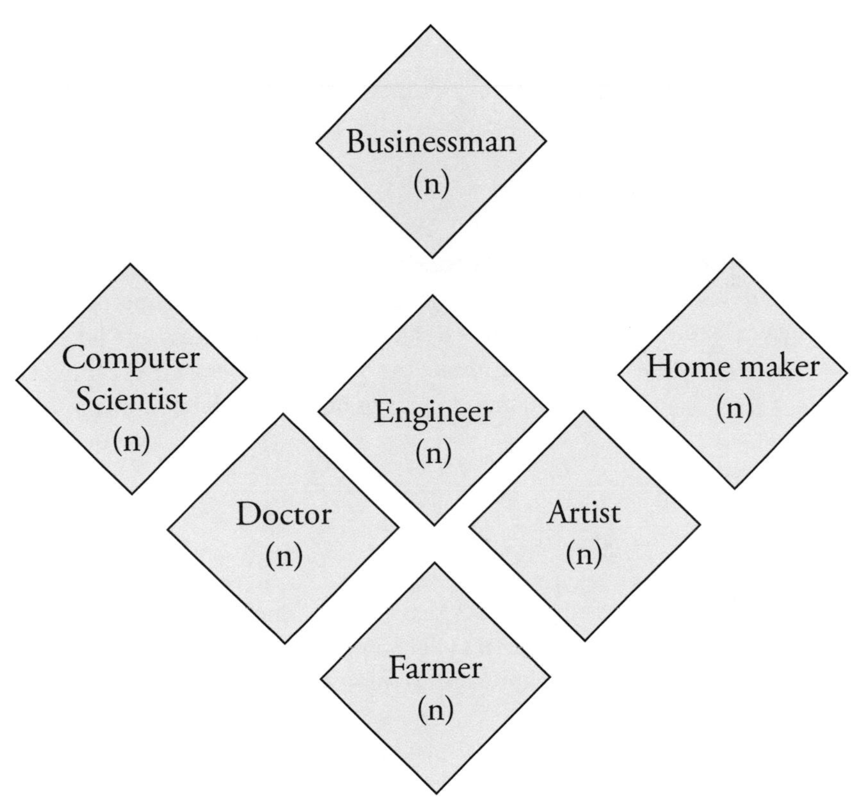

Figure 2.6 Shihana's Diamond Sequence

error with the simple present tense which the instructor may choose—or not—to correct. but provides explanation and justification for her sequencing choices. The position of homemaker is interesting and offers avenues for discussion and enables the rest of the class to compare and contrast their own diamond sequences with those of their classmates.

This activity can be used at all levels with more or less sophisticated vocabulary and more or less complex concepts depending on level:

- A1 topic: Jobs
- A2 topic: Leisure
- B1 topic: Environment
- B2 topic: Business
- C1 topic: Relationships

6. The Color Vowel® Vocabulary Warm-Up

✓ Levels A1-C1
✓ Online compatible

The **Color Vowel® Vocabulary Warm-Up** is a fantastic tool for practicing sounds of words, relating those sounds to the written word, using physical movement to reinforce length of vowel sound and primary stress, considering thought groups and intonation, providing relevant schemata, vocabulary, parts of speech, and a focus on morphology prior to reading a new text.

Link to Theory:

The Color Vowel® Vocabulary Warm-Up:

- contributes to reading fluency as it builds phonemic awareness through matching phonemes to graphemes;
- introduces schemata through vocabulary essential to new text comprehension;
- contributes to automaticity as new vocabulary is *heard*, then *seen*, then *recorded;*
- reduces cognitive overload by looking at a reduced amount of text and vocabulary *prior* to textbook matching exercises;
- identifies unusual spelling where phoneme to grapheme match *does not* reflect word pronunciation;
- enables students to notice emerging sound and spelling patterns as they record new vocabulary in the Color Vowel® Organizer;
- uses kinesthetic movement to reinforce sound and word stress;

- paves the way for discussion on definition, speech parts, and morphology;
- creates a record of all targeted vocabulary.

A Brief Explanation of the Color Vowel® Chart

The Color Vowel® Chart (Figure 2.7) created by Taylor and Thompson (2018) is a profile of the mouth with vowels placed according to position of tongue, jaw, and lips. Instead of using the IPA to teach the sounds of English through symbols, the Color Vowel® Chart uses color to denote sounds of vowels crucial to phonemic awareness, word comprehension, and reading automaticity and fluency. Instead of matching letter to sound in English—a language with confusing and irregular spelling—the Color Vowel® Chart links sound to color through an anchor phrase that demonstrates and reinforces each particular peak (stressed) vowel sound (Figure 2.8):

GREEN TEA /EE/; SILVER PIN /IH/; GRAY DAY /AY/, etc.

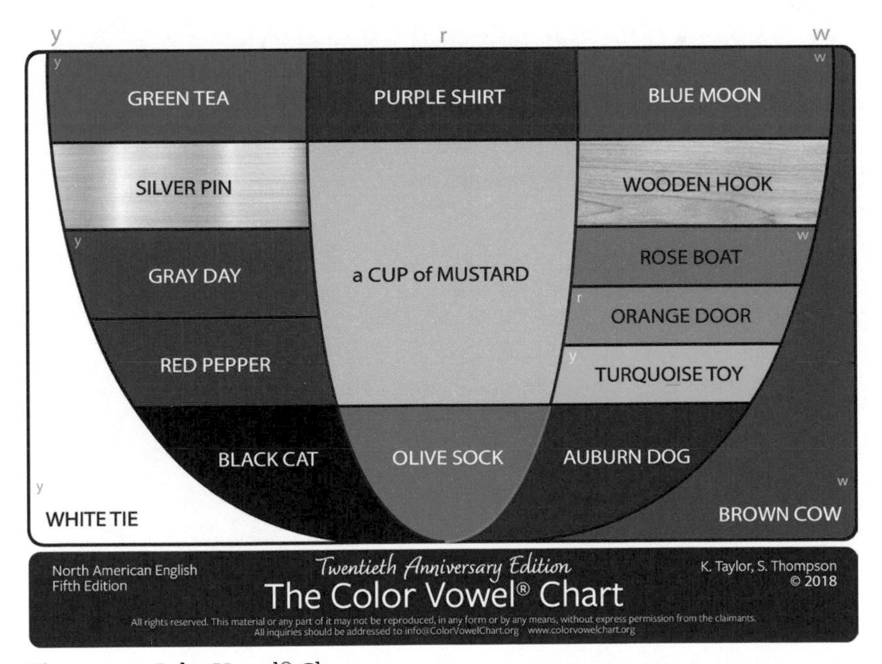

Figure 2.7 Color Vowel® Chart

Example Anchor Phrases followed by peak vowel sound and example vocabulary:

- GREEN TEA /EE/, GREEN TEA teacher
- SILVER PIN /IH/, SILVER PIN different
- GRAY DAY /AY/, GRAY DAY location
- RED PEPPER /EH/, RED PEPPER bread

For more explanation on Color Vowel®, go to **www.colorvowel.com**

Figure 2.8 Example Anchor Phrases Followed by Peak Vowel Sound and Example Vocabulary.

Position of Vowels on the Chart: what do the columns signify?

- The left side of the chart represents vowel sounds made at the front of the mouth.
- The middle column represents vowel sounds made in the middle area of the mouth:
- The colors to the right of the middle column represent vowels sounds made at the back of the mouth.
- BROWN COW is a moving vowel and begins close to AUBURN DOG and ends with BLUE MOON.
- WHITE TIE is a moving vowel and begins close to BLACK CAT and ends with GREEN TEA.

Position of Vowels on the Chart: what does the height position signify?

The height of the Color Vowel® represents the position of the jaw and tongue:

- GREEN TEA is made at the front of the mouth with the jaw and tongue high and lips spread.
- A CUP of MUSTARD is made in the middle of the mouth with jaw, tongue, and lips neutral.

- AUBURN DOG is made at the back of the mouth with the jaw and tongue low and the lips forward and rounded.
- The anchor phrases are read clockwise from GREEN TEA to BLUE MOON, then from a CUP of MUSTARD to PURPLE SHIRT, then to BROWN COW and finally WHITE TIE.

Procedure:

1. Elicit relevant vocabulary through a thunk; students are more knowledgeable than we realize, and it is very possible that new, targeted vocabulary may be familiar to some; this enables clarification of new vocabulary definitions before the warm-up itself.
   Important**:** at this stage, clarification of meaning should be oral and swift!
2. Say the target vocabulary twice followed by the anchor phrase and the target vocabulary once more.
   - pizza, pizza, GREEN TEA pizza
   - different, different SILVER PIN, different
   - bread, bread, RED PEPPER, bread
   - chat, chat**,** BLACK CAT, chat

   And so on . . .

   Important: As you pronounce each target word (or focus word), extend your arm to show the length of sound carried by the peak vowel (the primary stressed vowel in the word), and open your hand to indicate primary stress. This activates the areas of the brain associated with rhythm and movement. See examples on YouTube such as Blue Canoe Learning (2018).
3. Students repeat each word and anchor phrase after the instructor.
   Important: this is an oral exercise; even if students don't yet have a clear mental definition or image of the words, phonemically they are now ready to link phoneme to grapheme *despite*—not because of—spelling.
4. Introduce the new vocabulary words visually on the board and ask students to work in pairs to decide on primary stress and color; this ensures phonemic introduction and familiarity *before* written definition exercises and reading text are introduced.
5. Elicit meaning for each word. Identify any spellings that are different, but make the same sound: /types/ /rice/; elicit speech part for each

word and record on board; note morphological changes for different speech parts: /type/ (n) /typical/ (adj).

6. Ask students to record new vocabulary in their Color Vowel® Organizer in the correct color categories and underline the primary stress of each word.

Example Color Vowel® Vocabulary Warm-Up

You are about to begin a unit on food and culture and want to introduce your A1 students to vocabulary essential to a new text. You have introduced the topic through visuals or elicited schemata via a thunk; many of the new vocabulary words and phrases have come up in response to your thunk, and you are ready to formally introduce them now. Your excellent textbook has sentences with targeted vocabulary in bold together with a "match the word to the correct definition" exercise; the exercises introduce schemata and vocabulary, but the page is rather dense with text, the eye is drawn to vocabulary in bold *before* sentence context, and definitions are rather wordy. There is potential for cognitive overload: we might lose the student before we begin. Instead, let's do a Color Vowel® warm-up!

Stage 1: Thunk*: Which country makes the sweetest desserts?* The discussion elicits target vocabulary such as prepare; different; same; types; honey.

Stage 2: In order to build phonemic awareness, we want to:

- First, hear each new word/phrase pronounced with its primary stress. The new words are: honey; different; drinks; same; prepares; bread; types.
- Since the textbook introduces seven new words for this reading, we will create additional, topic-related words or phrases to complete the chart, and for ease of memory, will record them in the instructor's blank Color Vowel® Organizer.

Stage 3: Students repeat the target vocabulary and anchor phrase to build phonemic knowledge of new vocabulary.

Stage 4: Introduce the words visually on the board and identify color and primary stress for each word.

Stage 5: Elicit meaning for each word and identify any unusual spelling patterns (Figure 2.11).

Stage 6: Students record the new words honey; different; drinks; prepares; same; bread; types in their Color Vowel® Organizer. As they record more words, they will begin to notice new correlations between sound and spelling emerge.

COLOR VOWEL® Organizer (CVO)

GREEN TEA: pizza	WHITE TIE: types	BLUE MOON: spoon
SILVER PIN: Different, drinks	BROWN COW: now	WOODEN HOOK: put
		ROSE BOAT: show
GRAY DAY: Prepares, same	PURPLE SHIRT: first	ORANGE DOOR: fork
RED PEPPER: bread	a CUP of MUSTARD: honey	TURQUOISE TOY: enjoy
BLACK CAT: chat	OLIVE SOCK: hot	AUBURN DOG: log

Figure 2.9 Color Vowel® Organizer

This is a superb tool for *all* levels. The *hear; see; record* principle facilitates word storage in long-term memory which aids automaticity and fluency. The earlier students learn Color Vowel® methodology (Taylor et al., 2016), the stronger their phonemic awareness becomes, and the more this impacts

Vocabulary for A1 reading on Food and Culture. Underline denotes peak vowel with primary stress.

- honey
- different
- drinks
- same
- prepares
- bread
- types

Additional words chosen chosen to complete the sounds of the Color Vowel® Chart:

- pizza
- spoon
- put
- first
- show
- enjoy
- fork
- chat
- hot
- log

Figure 2.10 Target Vocabulary

pattern recognition and so develops reading fluency. I award credit for weekly inspection of the Color Vowel® Organizer (Taylor and Thompson, 2018); I check to see that new words have been recorded in the correct color box and that primary stress has been underlined correctly. Students love this method!

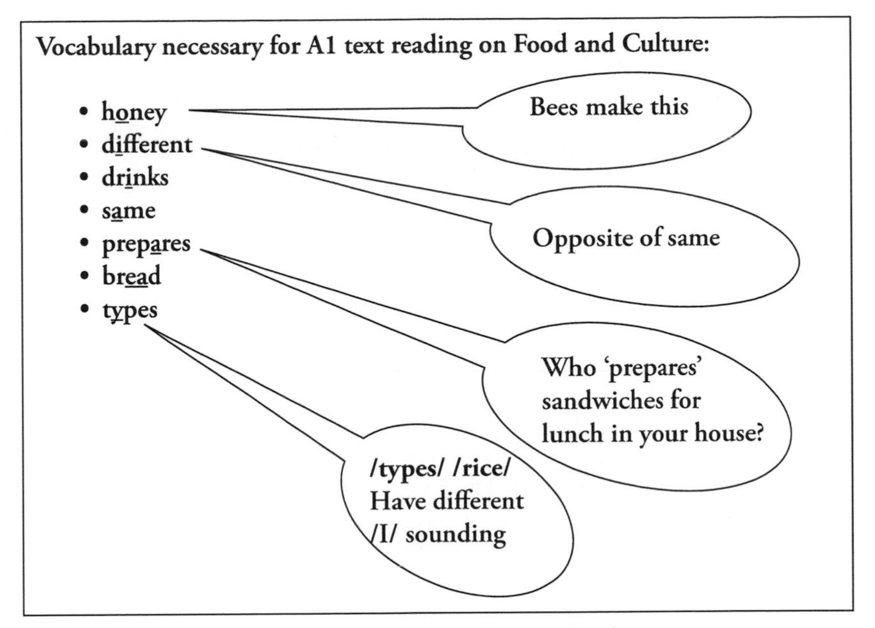

Figure 2.11 Vocabulary for A1 Reading on Food and Culture

It gives them a hook to hang both sound and reading on, an aid to pronunciation, and a visual relating to sound. A1 to C1 students use the method automatically, extend their arms for length of primary vowel, and open their hand to indicate peak vowel stress. It is reading with sound, visuals, and movement; together, they reinforce word meaning, structure, and pronunciation.

Chapter 3
Interactive Reading Activities

The process of reading is by definition an interactive process: the author has a message to convey, and the reader has the "job" of interpreting, inferring, and comprehending the message conveyed, and assimilating it into their own mental landscape of prior knowledge and personal experience (Gibbons, 2015; Smith et al., 2021). This process is a demanding one, especially when L2 learners are confronted with large volumes of text. In this chapter, we will introduce strategies to reduce overwhelm associated with large volumes of text, strategies for location and extraction of information, interpretation of information, and for B2 to C1 students, synthesis and critical evaluation of more than one text.

Each activity will guide students through a particular reading focus targeting different elements of comprehension and analysis. Instead of reading texts for gist, details, language, and analysis all at the same time, students will read strategically and purposefully. They will use different forms of annotation and writing frames and examine text collaboratively and individually. If Chapter 2 focused on schema theory, contributing to fluency through scaffolded access to new text, this chapter focuses on how to read for content, build automaticity, organize analysis, and most importantly, reduce the cognitive burden.

Strategic Reading 1: Top-Down Processing

- ✓ Levels A1 to C1
- ✓ Online compatible

Top-Down Processing involves reading for main ideas or abstract concepts. It is not a close analysis of text; instead, it involves a brief sweep of the reading rather than a word-by-word, phrase-by-phrase, and sentence-by-sentence analysis.

Karol, a bright C1 student, came to me in tears: "Aviva, I have five articles to read for ENC1101 for tomorrow [the basic college reading and writing course all freshmen must take]. I'm only on article number two, and it has 20 pages. How can I read so much?"

After a little digging, I realized the student was reading each article in its entirety! While Karol is to be applauded for her good intentions—and I'm sure the authors would be very grateful for the attention and due diligence she intended to give to each article—this is NOT strategic reading!

Link to Theory:

A short conversation later, Karol is introduced to **top-down processing** which enables her to:

- focus initially on key ideas and concepts;
- create a roadmap of the text with brief annotations in the margin;
- practice summary and paraphrase;
- reduce the volume of text requiring close reading and focus and so reduce cognitive overload;
- engage critical thinking skills through attention to genre and authorial source.

Procedure:

1. Determine the reading outcome as "reading for main ideas."
2. Determine text type from title and any graphics.
3. Determine author and annotate for any notable names or anything that might point to authorial stance.
4. Underline or highlight the topic sentences in each paragraph (for lengthy articles at the C1 level, do so for article abstract, introduction, and conclusion).
5. Annotate in the margin a brief comment on content of section or paragraph.

Example of Top-Down Processing

The annotated text overleaf shows an example of top-down processing where the most important ideas or information are highlighted, and a short annotation in the margin is written to remind the reader of the main paragraph point (see Figure 3.1). Students should automatically highlight and annotate to create a roadmap of the text's key points.

	B2 Informational **Text: Informatioal text about Latin-American Art in Boca?** **Controlling Idea** **Authors?** **A LATIN AMERICAN EXTRAVAGANZA AT THE BOCA RATON MUSEUM OF ART/IEI Faculty 2022**
Art museum in Boca Raton focuses on Latin American art.	Did you know that Boca Raton has its own art museum right off the beautiful Mizner Boulevard? It is called the Boca Museum of Art and its hosts multiple exhibitions throughout the year. Many exhibitioners focus on modern art, sculpture, ceramics, and fine arts. You can view new masterpieces, originals, and reprints of classic photographs or paintings along the gallery halls during during opening hours. Most importantly, the museum opens a window to Latin American art in all its complexity and beauty.
Local, national, and international artists from Latin America.	In addition to local and nationally recognized artists, the museum showcases international artists from Latin America. Recently, the museum held an exploration of Machu Pichu and Peruvian Art. Displays of indegenous creations, bowls, sculptures, and clothes used for Inca worship drew visitors from local schools, colleges, and from the whole of South Florida. It was a strikingly beautiful exhibition with rave reviews from professionals and regular visitors alike.
Civil rights through art?	Other events and exhibitions have showcased themes focusing on civil rights. With indegenous art and decolonization of art a focus, and with emphasis on social justice movements, the museum draws inspiration from local Latin American groups, the politics and history of Brazil, Cuba, and Peru, to Latin American fashions and culture of modern times. While Boca Raton is diverse in population, the large community of Spanish speaking residents makes an interest in art from Latin America an important feature of the museum's exhibitions.
Education and community program.	The museum is also committed to community involvement and interaction through its education program. This program opens the doors to elementary, middle, and high school students, provides classes in painting and photography, and art lectures to interested parties. If you visit the museum during opening hours, you will see children sitting cross-legged on the floor sketching a sculpture, adults strolling through the galleries, and professionals enjoying a short break from their offices nearby.
Important place to visit in Boca Raton.	All in all, the Boca Raton Museum of Art is a wonderful place to stop and view a vivid exploration of Latin American art. It provides community outreach, education, and forms a center for Latin American art history second to none in South Florida. Situated at the top of the Mizner Boulevard, it is surrounded by chic boutiques, high-end restaurants, and lies a stone throw away from the beautiful Boca Raton coast. A trip to Boca Raton is not complete without a visit to the Boca Raton Museum of Art.

Figure 3.1 Strategic Reading 1: Top-Down Processing

Stage 1: Reading outcome on board: *Reading for main ideas of text, A Latin American Extravaganza at the Boca Raton Museum of Art.*

Stage 2: Text type identified as informational text which means the authors intend to provide information on the museum, and possibly provide opinions and reviews of the museum.

Stage 3: Author is IEI Faculty 2022—authorial stance unclear (though teacher Aviva has waxed lyrical about the museum before, and this suggests a pro-museum bias).

Stage 4: Topic sentences highlighted in yellow so roadmap of main ideas easily viewed at a glance.

Stage 5: Each paragraph annotated with brief comment on paragraph content:

- Paragraph 1: Art museum in Boca Raton focuses on Latin American art.
- Paragraph 2: Local, national, and international artists from Latin American.
- Paragraph 3: Civil rights through art?
- Paragraph 4: Education and community program.
- Paragraph 5: Important place to visit in Boca.

Instead of laboring through a 422-word article, students focus on the 105 words highlighted in yellow. Since we read in a series of fixations and jumps, but regress or look backwards at words and phrases we cannot immediately understand, reducing the number of words reduces the number of fixations, jumps, regressions, and so reduces intensive labor. The reading rate increases, which is both antecedent to, and the result of fluency. Since our *top-down processing* intends to note the general concepts introduced in the text, and since our own prior knowledge and experience of such topics help to predict what the text might include, we reduce the volume of text, focus on main ideas, create a textual roadmap, and reduce the cognitive burden with a few small strokes of the pen or annotation highlighter!

This automatic highlighting should be done at all levels. Beginning with A1 and simple text, highlighting topic sentences and main ideas is key. Once the habit is ingrained, it creates a working strategy utilized at each level as the student progresses. Margin annotation should also be encouraged from A2 upwards. Even a question mark or one word in the margin of a multi-paragraph text creates a roadmap and, in doing so, reduces the reading cognitive burden.

Strategic Reading 2: Bottom-Up Processing

✓ Levels A1 to C1
✓ Online compatible

Bottom-up processing involves decoding each word at morphological level, syntactic level, and parsing of meaning. It involves working memory capacity, and the more laborious the decoding, the less room there is for critical thinking skills such as analysis, synthesis, and evaluation. However, in order to expand word recognition and its long-term memory storage, and in order to facilitate automatic retrieval, our students *have* to encounter language they do not recognize. In doing so, they infer meaning from context, morphology, and syntax, and move from general concept to specific details.

Link to Theory:

Bottom-up processing enables students to:

- make connections and notice patterns;
- practice automaticity;
- access their own mental lexicon and semantic fields;
- link old schemata to new contexts;
- practice phonemic awareness;
- practice top-down processing and bottom-up processing simultaneously.

Procedure:

1. Instruct the students to circle/underline unfamiliar words and concepts.
2. Instruct students to "notice" patterns, connections, links to schemata, and mark the text with arrows, underline, circle, highlight, etc.
3. Continue to build phonemic awareness by identifying primary vowel stress and word color.
4. Discuss with the whole class and annotate on the board.
5. Link bottom-up processing to general concepts and ideas from initial top-down processing activity.

Example of Bottom-Up Processing

Let's imagine our student is tasked with focusing on exhibits of social justice at the Boca Raton Museum of Art. Which paragraph does the student go to?

Paragraph 3, of course. The student already knows where to locate the information as they have previously highlighted the topic sentences in each paragraph and annotated the margins to create an easily accessible road map. Now, however, students need to read more "closely" and use bottom-up reading skills to gather more detailed information. In this short paragraph, the reader must contend with words such as "indigenous," "decolonization," "diverse," and the concepts of "civil rights" and "social justice": not an easy task!

Stage 1: Students underline or circle unfamiliar words or phrases such as indigenous, decolonization, diverse, and social justice movements.
Stage 2: Students annotate text using arrows and question marks to indicate queries on language or content (see Figure 3.2).
Stage 3: Students build phonemic awareness and analyze unfamiliar vocabulary.
Stage 4: Students link details to main ideas identified in top-down processing.
Stage 5: Annotate on board with student input.

> Ok, class: can we break down the word "decolonization"? Svetlana says "de" and "colonization"? Great. What do we mean by the verb "colonize," by the way? Santiago? When a foreign power controls a country. Ok. So, if we "decolonize"? Olga? Take the foreign power away. "De." To take away. Great. So, if we are talking about decolonization of art, what does that mean for the indigenous people, the people

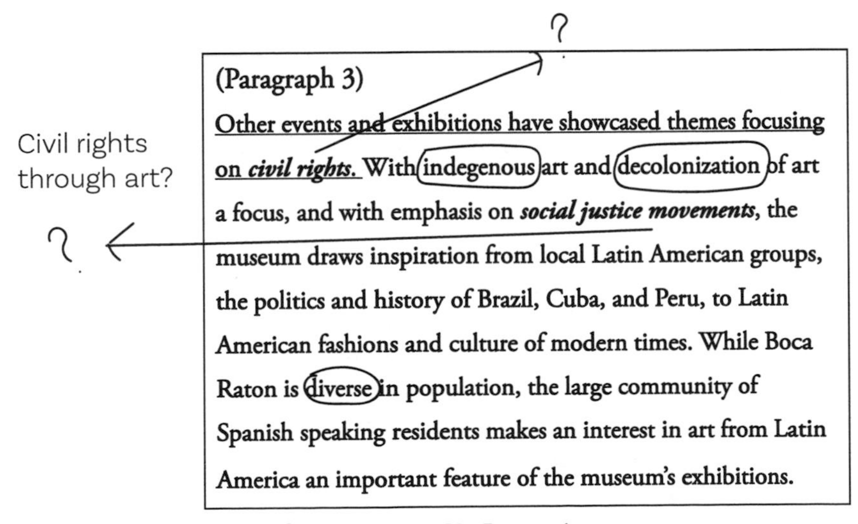

(Paragraph 3)

Other events and exhibitions have showcased themes focusing on *civil rights*. With indegenous art and decolonization of art a focus, and with emphasis on *social justice movements*, the museum draws inspiration from local Latin American groups, the politics and history of Brazil, Cuba, and Peru, to Latin American fashions and culture of modern times. While Boca Raton is diverse in population, the large community of Spanish speaking residents makes an interest in art from Latin America an important feature of the museum's exhibitions.

Figure 3.2 Strategic Reading 2: Bottom-Up Processing

that were there before—can anyone find a word to substitute for "indigenous"? Yes, well done, Muhammad! We could indeed substitute the word "native" and the sentence would retain its meaning.

What about color and stress? Decolonization (n) (GRAY DAY); and the verb? Decolonize (v) OLIVE. Fantastic. And indigenous (adj)? Yup. SILVER PIN. Excellent.

What about "diverse"? Diverse (n) (PURPLE SHIRT). What speech part is it? Thank you, Bojanna, it's an adjective. What could we substitute for "diverse population"?

"a nice population"? I'm sure it is, but that doesn't retain the original meaning of the sentence. The population is very "different"? Interesting. What do you mean by "different," Pedro?

Ah, there are many different nationalities in Boca Raton. The connective "While" suggests a contrast to the specific Latin American community. People come from different backgrounds . . . Excellent. So, what do we mean by "diverse"? "Different," a "variety," thank you Clara.

*Does anyone notice anything about the form of the word diverse? How do we create the noun here? Diversit***y***. Excellent. Any other words you can think of that we can add a "y" to create a noun? Active—activit***y***! Nice one, Saud.*

Any other unfamiliar words? Oh yes: "showcased." Stress and color? Correct: (ROSE BOAT) for both verb and noun. Well, what patterns can you see? Or what words can you see within this word? Right. Show and case? You can see a show in a case? What kind of case? A suitcase?

No. That's right, Victor: a glass cabinet, or perhaps even just a space on the wall which shows off a piece of art.

And what speech part does the writer use for "showcased" in this paragraph?

Right. Here it's a verb—we can tell because of the subject before and the -ed ending. But we can also use "showcase" as a noun. What other word here suggests a showcase? We talked about this before. Think of how we show pictures. Yes, Svetlana: we "portray a picture," we show a picture. Anyone remember the noun for the verb to portray? "Portrait!" Portrait meaning a picture of someone.

See, you don't need to understand each and every word to make sense of the material; and even if you are missing key words, try and substitute a word and see if the sentence makes sense, or deconstruct the word and see if you can find patterns or mini-words within it to help you understand.

What about these concepts you've underlined? Civil rights and social justice movements.

Civil rights. Stress and Color? Civil rights: WHITE TIE. Remember there is only one focus word in your phrase or collocation.

Can anyone think of any similar or connected words? Nice, Felix, civilization? What do we mean by "civilization"?

Okay, people. Organized society. Fantastic. Anyone know the root of civilization/civil?

Any classics scholars in the classroom? Yes, Felix? Right! It's Latin for citizen. Civis.

*So, we've already talked about colonization, or decolonization—showcasing art made by native people—so if we're talking about civil rights, together with social (adj)—society (n)—*rights *(n), then what does the museum exhibit or like to exhibit? Absolutely, Olga, rights of the people. Justice for the people.*

What about movement? How does that relate to "social justice"? A social justice movement? [Always extend arm and open hand to indicate stress.] *Yes, Ali, move is a verb, but movement is a noun. Well spotted.*

So, what does move mean? To make progress? Not to stay in one place? Take action, even. Fantastic!

So, if we turn that into a noun and link it to social justice, what do we think a "social justice movement" might mean?

Ali, you are correct yet again! A group that takes social justice forward, fights for social justice.

Stage 6. How does the focus on indigenous art link to the main purpose of the text? Why is it important to reflect Latin American art in a South Florida museum?

In one short(ish) conversation, your students have deconstructed, substituted, noticed, and explained away unfamiliar vocabulary with just a little prompting from you!

This activity can and should be done at all levels. A1 to C1 students should circle, underline, annotate with question marks, arrows, anything to indicate they are thinking about the text, focusing on both general concepts and the minutiae of words and their constructs. The exciting part is that once students become proficient at bottom-up processing, top-down and bottom-up processing work simultaneously and free up working memory for analysis and critical thinking. As students become more aware of morphological and syntactic patterns, their ability to infer from context improves, as does automatic retrieval of meaning from their long-term memory storage.

Strategic Reading 3: Jigsaw Technique

✓ Levels A1 to C1
✓ Online compatible

There are many excellent textbooks on the market with text and questions carefully crafted to help students locate and extract, infer and deduce, and evaluate and synthesize information. The aim of this book is not to revisit tried and tested techniques, but to reduce the learning burden caused by large volumes of text, unfamiliar vocabulary, and unfamiliar schemata, and suggest how to help students dissect a text with particular goals in mind. With that being the case, let's look at how we can encourage close reading of larger texts with structure and discourse as the main focus.

Link to Theory:

The **jigsaw technique** enables students to:

- focus on one part of a text closely and reduce cognitive burden;
- focus on discourse and structure through connectives, transition signals, and links to the general content;
- access schemata necessary for whole-text comprehension;
- practice critical thinking skills;
- work collaboratively and communicatively.

Procedure:

1. Divide your class into groups of two to four students.
2. Divide your text into paragraphs and ask each pair/group of students to focus on their specific paragraph and do the following:
   - Underline/highlight the topic sentence and identify the topic and controlling idea: what is the sentence about, and where does the writer want to take you with this topic?
   - Annotate in the margin: what is the main idea of the paragraph in one phrase or sentence?
   - Circle any discourse markers or transition signals suggesting comparison or contrast and label their function.

3. Once each group reads their paragraph, highlights the topic sentence, and finds the relevant discourse markers or transition signals, it is time for the class to sequence *all* the paragraphs together and tape them to the board based on textual clues.
4. It is now time for a spokesperson from each group to summarize their paragraph orally, indicate the topic and controlling idea, identify the discourse markers for comparison/contrast, and explain how they found their place within the essay as a whole.
5. While each group explains their thought process, a hard copy of the whole essay may be distributed to the class, and annotations take place as students explain their work.

Example of the Jigsaw Technique

Your B1 students are going to read a text focusing on comparison and contrast. It is a lengthy text, and you want to ensure that vocabulary and structure for comparison and contrast remain central to this reading. The text itself is not particularly difficult, but time is short and while the content is worthy of discussion, you really want students looking at connections between paragraphs and within sentences. The **jigsaw technique** looks like this (see Figure 3.3):

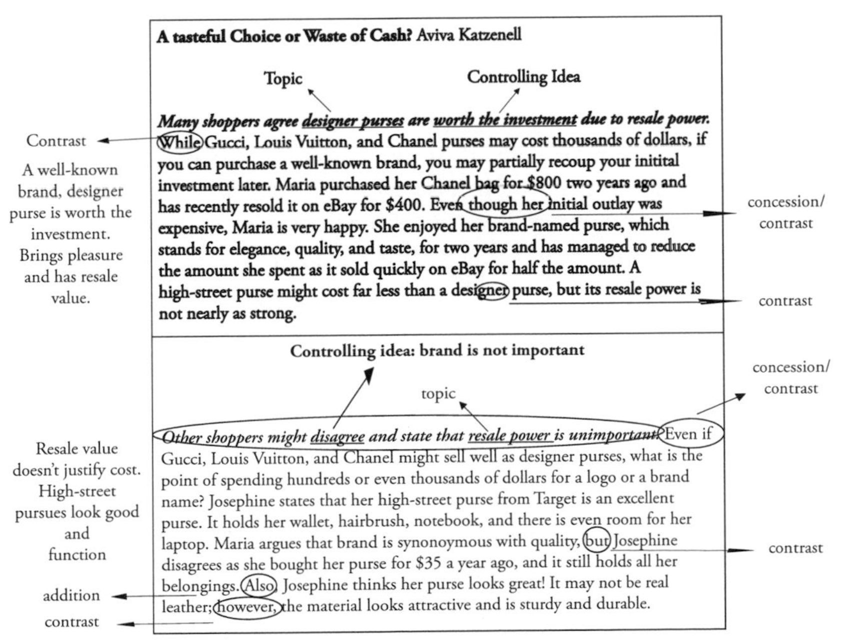

A tasteful Choice or Waste of Cash? Aviva Katzenell

Many shoppers agree designer purses are worth the investment due to resale power. **While Gucci, Louis Vuitton, and Chanel purses may cost thousands of dollars, if you can purchase a well-known brand, you may partially recoup your initital investment later. Maria purchased her Chanel bag for $800 two years ago and has recently resold it on eBay for $400. Even though her initial outlay was expensive, Maria is very happy. She enjoyed her brand-named purse, which stands for elegance, quality, and taste, for two years and has managed to reduce the amount she spent as it sold quickly on eBay for half the amount. A high-street purse might cost far less than a designer purse, but its resale power is not nearly as strong.**

Other shoppers might disagree and state that resale power is unimportant. Even if Gucci, Louis Vuitton, and Chanel might sell well as designer purses, what is the point of spending hundreds or even thousands of dollars for a logo or a brand name? Josephine states that her high-street purse from Target is an excellent purse. It holds her wallet, hairbrush, notebook, and there is even room for her laptop. Maria argues that brand is synonoymous with quality, but Josephine disagrees as she bought her purse for $35 a year ago, and it still holds all her belongings. Also Josephine thinks her purse looks great! It may not be real leather; however, the material looks attractive and is sturdy and durable.

Figure 3.3 Strategic Reading 3: The Jigsaw Technique

Stages 1–3: Topic sentences highlighted, paragraphs annotated, paragraphs sequenced.
Stages 4–5: Students present their work and whole-class annotations on essay commence.

Students should be aware of English text conventions and will identify the paragraph with the title as the first in the sequence; the group with paragraph 2 should, in discussion with the paragraph 1 group, identify that the topic sentence in paragraph 2 is in direct contrast to the topic sentence in paragraph 1, and that the second paragraph attempts to refute the content of the first paragraph. Students with remaining paragraphs will follow similar logic until the entire essay is sequenced on the board (with white tac or tape, or on a digital whiteboard via Zoom). The instructor can address any mistakes in sequencing as the process occurs.

Depending on additional essay focus, the students may well have to read the essay as a whole. However, the initial skills of identifying topic sentence, topic and controlling idea, summarizing of the paragraph's key idea, and identifying discourse markers for comparison and contrast has been carried out without overwhelming text volume. Additionally, moving around the classroom, or viewing the different paragraphs via Google Docs and Zoom, looking at others' topic sentences, content summaries, and concluding sentences provides students with sequencing skills and activates critical thinking skills. There is no need to read each and every word in each and every paragraph in order to sense where each group's paragraph belongs. What can be done as macro, has been carried out in micro with a lower cognitive burden.

This exercise can be adapted for A1 and A2 classes with a focus on identifying topic sentence, key verbs, adjectives, nouns, adverbs, tense, or any other focal language point. It is useful for identifying referents at lower levels and making connections between one sentence and another.

Strategic Reading 4: Synthesis and Evaluation

- ✓ Levels B1 to C1
- ✓ Online compatible

Students intending to further their academic careers at undergraduate level in the United States are required to do a college reading and writing class. At Florida Atlantic University, this course is called ENC 1101 and includes essay structure, quotation, in-text citation, synthesis of articles, evaluation, and bibliography. In order to prepare students for reading and studying in an L2 at this level, we need to focus on carefully scaffolded, strategic reading.

Link to Theory:

Synthesis and evaluation helps students:

- identify the main idea of the article, paraphrase, and record it in an organized fashion;
- extract key quote(s) for students' use in the essay;
- activate critical thinking skills;
- guide students to produce a general hypothesis based on an initial strategic reading;
- cite sources so they are found easily should the student want to revisit a particular article;
- practice reference and bibliography skills.

Procedure:

1. Provide students with a table to organize and collect information.
2. Instruct students to cite sources in relevant format (Modern Language Association [MLA]; American Psychological Association [APA]), and do so alphabetically.
3. Instruct students to summarize the key idea of an article by examining the abstract and conclusion using top-down and bottom-up processing skills; Instruct students to record relevant quotes from each article.
4. Instruct students to include their own brief commentary in the column for "My Thoughts."
5. Instruct students to look for additional articles using the library and Google Scholar.
6. Instruct students to compose a general hypothesis based on a first sweep of three articles.

Example of Synthesis and Evaluation

Remember our bright, but disorganized C1 student from Strategic Reading No. 1? Karol now has to write an essay on reading skills for her intensive

English writing class. She has been given two articles to read and has been asked to source another one independently. Karol is perfectly able, but faced with two articles of several pages in length and the need to source additional articles independently, she requires structure to organize both reading and thought process.

The essay question:

> In Shakespeare's play Romeo and Juliet, Juliet states: "What's in a name? A rose by any other name would smell as sweet." What does it mean to "know" a word? Do you think Juliet's statement is correct?

Fortunately, Karol knows how to employ top-down and bottom-up processing skills. She is now adept at highlighting key ideas, roadmap annotation in the margin, inferring meaning from context, and linking ideas through in-text annotation. Her class has discussed the notion of "names" and read Juliet's "What's in a name" speech from Romeo and Juliet, Act II, Scene II, and she is ready to complete her table. This involves citation for each article, extracting the key idea from each article, and finding a usable quote from each article too. In the column headed "My Thoughts," Karol includes her own evaluation of each article in reference to her essay question. Using strategic reading techniques 1 to 4, Karol has read strategically, organized her material thoughtfully, generated an overall hypothesis, and is ready for bottom-up processing of the relevant sections in each article; ultimately, she is ready to read and ready to write!

Stage 1: Table provided (see Table 3.1).
Stage 2: Sources cited in "Source" column.
Stage 3: Key idea of each article briefly summarized in "Key Idea" column; relevant quote from each article recorded in "Quote and Page" column.
Stage 4: Karol's brief thought on article content recorded in "My Thoughts" column.
Stage 5: Karol has carried out a Google Scholar and Florida Atlantic University Library search for relevant articles.
Stage 6: Karol has recorded a general hypothesis based on stages 1 to 5.

This exercise can be carried out at B1 to C1 levels. Any task involving one or more articles requiring quotation, citation, and critical evaluation needs an organizational structure and a clear table to record the different elements. This table can also be adjusted for A2 to B1 levels focusing on main ideas, supporting details, and the students' own thoughts. Our students are bright, thoughtful, and full of ideas; a structured table facilitates thought process and prompts crucial critical thinking skills.

Table 3.1 Strategic Reading 4: Synthesis and Evaluation

Source	Key Idea	Quote and Page	My Thoughts
Baldwin, Emma. "A rose by any other name would smell as sweet." Poem Analysis, https://poemanalvsis.com/shakespeare-quotes/a-rose-by-any-other-name-would-smell-as-sweet/. Accessed 1 October 2022.	*Shakespeare uses this quote within Romeo and Juliet as a way of asking readers and theater audiences to consider the meaning of names. What role do names play in everyday life, and what power do they have?*	*"What control, she wonders, does it have over the object or person it's attached to? [Juliet] deduces that it has no real control, only that which people are willing to give to it."*	Words, names have meaning and also tell us where we come from and who we are. In a global world, we need everyone to identify the meaning of a name and a word. It is not random . . .
Laufer, Batia. "What percentage of text-lexis is essential for comprehension?" Special language: From humans thinking to thinking machines (1989).	*Vocabulary acquisition is vital for second language learners*	*"In the field of Reading for Specific Purposes ... the most serious difficulties that foreign learners experience are lexical. This is so because text interpretation was found to be dependent mainly on the lexical and conceptual clues . . ."*	Without knowing words and their meanings, L2 learners cannot understand technical language.

(Continued)

Table 3.1 *Continued*

Source	Key Idea	Quote and Page	My Thoughts
Nation, Paul, and Robert Waring. "Vocabulary size, text coverage, and word lists." Vocabulary: Description, acquisition and pedagogy 14 (1997): 6–19.	*Examines the amount of vocabulary a learner has to know to function in a language*	*"Vocabulary knowledge enables language use, language use enables the increase of vocabulary knowledge, knowledge of the world enables the increase of vocabulary knowledge and language use and so on . . ."*	If vocab knowledge is essential then "knowing a word" must be important. Just calling an object by a name that is not recognized by anyone else is not helpful!
General hypothesis generated from examination of the three articles	*For second language learners it is especially important to "know" words and understand their definition. Shakespeare's romantic notion that a "rose by any other name would smell as sweet" helps Juliet to imagine her and Romeo together, but it is not practical, and in losing a name, we lose genuine meaning. Words, names and their meanings are not random!*		

Chapter 4
Post-reading Activities

For L2 learners, reading a text can be an end in itself; however, most readings are carried out in preparation for discussion of vocabulary, grammar, and concept. Once the reading is done, the real work begins: facilitation of automaticity, critical thinking skills, and schemata take place through discussion, exercises, and consolidation both in and out of the classroom. Here are a few of the most useful post-reading activities we can adapt to different levels:

1. The Cloze Exercise

- ✓ Levels A1 to C1
- ✓ Online compatible

Very often we use the **cloze exercise** as an in-class exercise, test, or exam option. Publishers provide excellent cloze structures and students enjoy the challenge such cloze exercises pose. It is worth, however, considering *how* and *whether* the cloze is useful for practice and consolidation, especially at the A1 and A2 levels, or whether it serves as a gap-fill without clear purpose. Applied appropriately, the cloze exercise is a useful tool. While we think we read in a linear fashion, what happens if a word is missing? How do our students fill in the gaps of knowledge if they do not "jump" forwards and backwards in a series of regressions and saccades?

Link to Theory:

This back and forth in a cloze exercise serves to:

- build eye tracking speed through practice and speed up reading rate;
- build automaticity and fluency dependent on context, morphology, and syntax;
- "notice" first person, third person, plurals, parts of speech, transitions, etc.;
- make connections between context, form, and function.

Procedure:

1. Prepare a cloze exercise based on student learning outcomes and teaching points. Gibbons (2015) suggests removal of every seventh or eighth word.
2. Ensure clues to missing words are based on lexis, morphology, syntax, and recognizable schemata.
3. Provide a word bank and ensure words fit grammatically into gaps in order to utilize morphological, grammatical, and syntactic knowledge, and so build automaticity and fluency.
4. Instruct your students to carry out the exercise in pairs to facilitate discussion.
5. Provide whole-class feedback with focus on why a particular word fits a gap as opposed to any other.

Example Cloze Exercise

Figure 4.1 gives an example of a cloze exercise with a focus on high beginner grammar and high beginner vocabulary on topics such as the classroom and friendship.

Word Bank							
Arabic	*in*	*is*	*from*	*study*	*speaks*	*friends*	*speak*

I am a student from Saudi Arabia. I ____________ English at Florida Atlantic University. I speak ______________ with my family and my friends. My teacher asks us to speak English ___ class. My friend Oleg is from Russia and __________ Russian. I also have ______________ from Peru in class and they ________ Spanish. It ____________ great to meet so many students from all over the world. I know I will make good progress if I speak English to all my new friends.

Figure 4.1 Cloze Exercise Example

Stage 1: Cloze exercise with a focus on high beginner grammar and vocabulary on learning English and friendship is provided.
Stage 2: Grammatical cues for correct use of present simple and content cues are given: *I (speak) English in the classroom. My friend Oleg is from Russian and (speak**s**) Russian.*
Stage 3: The word bank provides the correct forms of vocabulary; this enables high beginner students to fill in the blanks using lexical, morphological, and content clues.
Stage 4: Students fill in the blanks using the word bank provide in pairs. Pair work is important as it facilitates peer-to-peer discussion about why certain words fit particular blanks in a sentence.
Stage 5: Conduct whole class feedback and discussion:

Ok, Carlos, what word have you and Eduardo put in blank no. 1?Study. Excellent, why? You are absolutely correct Carlos. The sentence begins with the pronoun "I" and needs a verb immediately after. "Speaks" doesn't work because it needs a "he/she/it." The context suggests you are a student; "speak" could work grammatically, but "study" makes more sense.

Well done, guys. Fantastic work!

This exercise works beautifully for all levels from A1 to C1. While the cloze exercise may seem simple, it provides practice for a myriad of skills: students engage the physiological tracking process as the eye jumps from word to gap to word, and in doing so, they practice automaticity and engage long-term or working memory depending on skill level; students also consider appropriate speech part, syntax, and meaning to fill the gap. With both first and last sentences complete and providing logical context to the gap-fill choices, students access passage schemata and activate knowledge to help fill in the gaps. Finally, this is an excellent opportunity to practice basic vocabulary and grammar at the lower levels and use of sophisticated grammar and vocabulary at the upper levels.

2. Vocabulary Logs

- ✓ Levels A1 to C1
- ✓ Online compatible

Vocabulary logs are a great way to assist students in "knowing" a word or a phrase. They have completed reading their text, but there are certain words or phrases you'd like your students to focus on, or even better, there are certain words or phrases your students would like to investigate: they may be words that "tickle" them phonemically (they like the sounds and rhythm), or students may be puzzled by meaning or construct of a word and feel that they are "important" and merit more "work"; vocabulary may be familiar, but justifies additional investigation due to collocations or usage.

Link to Theory:

Forming a weekly, textual-based vocabulary log serves to:

- encourage phonemic awareness essential for reading skills;
- expand vocabulary usage;
- promote awareness of speech parts, morphology, and syntax;
- promote automaticity and fluency;
- promote creativity and choice.

Procedure

1. Design a functional log that makes sense to both students and instructors. Logs need to include relevant categories to ensure word and phrase knowledge. Anything from a simple table looking at definition, synonyms, antonyms, speech part, collocation, and usage within a sentence will do. However, an attractively designed vocabulary log provides incentive, a visual space where all information is available at a glance, and provides a means of simple collection or appraisal by the instructor.
2. After reading your text(s) for the week, instruct students to choose two to three words, or two words and a phrase for investigation.
3. Collect weekly, and award points for completion.
4. Discuss particularly interesting examples in class, with a focus on etymology, morphology, speech parts, definition, related words, and usage.

Example Vocabulary Logs

At the IEI at Florida Atlantic University, we currently have three vocabulary logs in service:

1. Our lower-level students benefit from using the Color Vowel® Organizer (Figure 4.2) as their weekly vocabulary log. They require phonemic practice and need to see different patterns of spelling originating from the same sounds, and discuss meaning, part of speech, morphology, and usage in class. Since we introduce

COLOR VOWEL® Organizer (CVO)

GREEN TEA
ingredients, increase, convenience, sequence, polyphenols, repeal, concrete, equal, delete, succeed

WHITE TIE
hybrid, biodiesel, acquire, hibernation, required, skylight vital, describe, (discribe)

BLUE MOON
pursue, fluid, commute, inuitive, construe, mutual, uniform, muse, ensue, institutional, scrutinize

SILVER PIN
discount, consider, influence, Italy, typical, persistance, disciplines, symbols, distributive, rhythm, rid, committed

BROWN COW
lounge, mount, count, counterpart, counterpane, devout, vouch, downy

WOODEN HOOK
book, cook

ROSE BOAT
mortgage, oriented, devoted, opposed, does, proponents

GRAY DAY
ratio, observations, brain, vocational, convey, eightieth, eightyrelation, negotiation

PURPLE SHIRT
sure, secure, learning, alternative, disturbing, verdict, prayer, burger dirt, rehearsal

ORANGE DOOR
adore, oriental, warn, core, sore, priorities

RED PEPPER
relatively, specialty, percentages, embarrass, generously, legend, envelope, weapon, fair

a CUP of MUSTARD
rummage, upload, truck, accustom, puppy, funded, substances, plum

TURQUOISE TOY
soybean

BLACK CAT
multinational, establish, bankruptcy, harass, Algebra, bandwidth, manual, advances

OLIVE SOCK
concrete, popular, launch, evolves, complex, involve, dropout, poppy, object

AUBURN DOG
launch, evolves

Figure 4.2 Vocabulary categorized in Color Vowel® Organizer

a maximum of eight new words per session, students avoid cognitive overload. Once color boxes are "full," we use Color Vowel® methodology to explore the different spellings of a sound. Instructors collect these logs on a weekly basis and award grades for completion.

2. B1 to B2 reading, writing, grammar students use the Word Cloud Log (see Figure 4.3) designed by Professor Zak Radd from the IEI at Florida Atlantic University. It includes clouds for:
    - words, and a third section includes a bubble for a phrase;
    - phonemic awareness: word color and primary stress;
    - definition;
    - synonym, antonym, and semantic field when relevant;
    - part of speech;
    - usage in a phrase or sentence.

    If, as Nation (2022) suggests, "knowing a word" and storing it in long-term memory to encourage automaticity and fluency involves knowing its constituent parts, then this design works beautifully. It is simple, attractive, yet it offers space to record just enough information to add knowledge without causing cognitive overload.
3. Our C1 reading, writing, and grammar students choose their own vocabulary log design, and as the examples in Figures 4.4 and 4.5 suggest, they invest time and effort into making their vocabulary logs meaningful and attractive. They favor mind-maps with the relevant breakdowns of information available at a glance; the use of humor, illustrations, and color provide extra links to long-term memory storage and make retrieval of focus words and phrases that much easier, not to mention fun for the instuctor!

All speaking, listening, and pronunciation students from A1 to C1 use the Color Vowel® Organizer to record vocabulary in both reading, writing, grammar, and in speaking, listening, and pronunciation classes. Students keep the Color Vowel® Organizer available on their desks and record new vocabulary as a matter of course. Upper-level students use additional logs for deeper word investigation and students take great pride in the volume of vocabulary recorded and presentation. If at the beginning of the term the answer to the question "what is vital to your language learning?" tends to be grammar, by the end of the term, the answer is indubitably vocabulary.

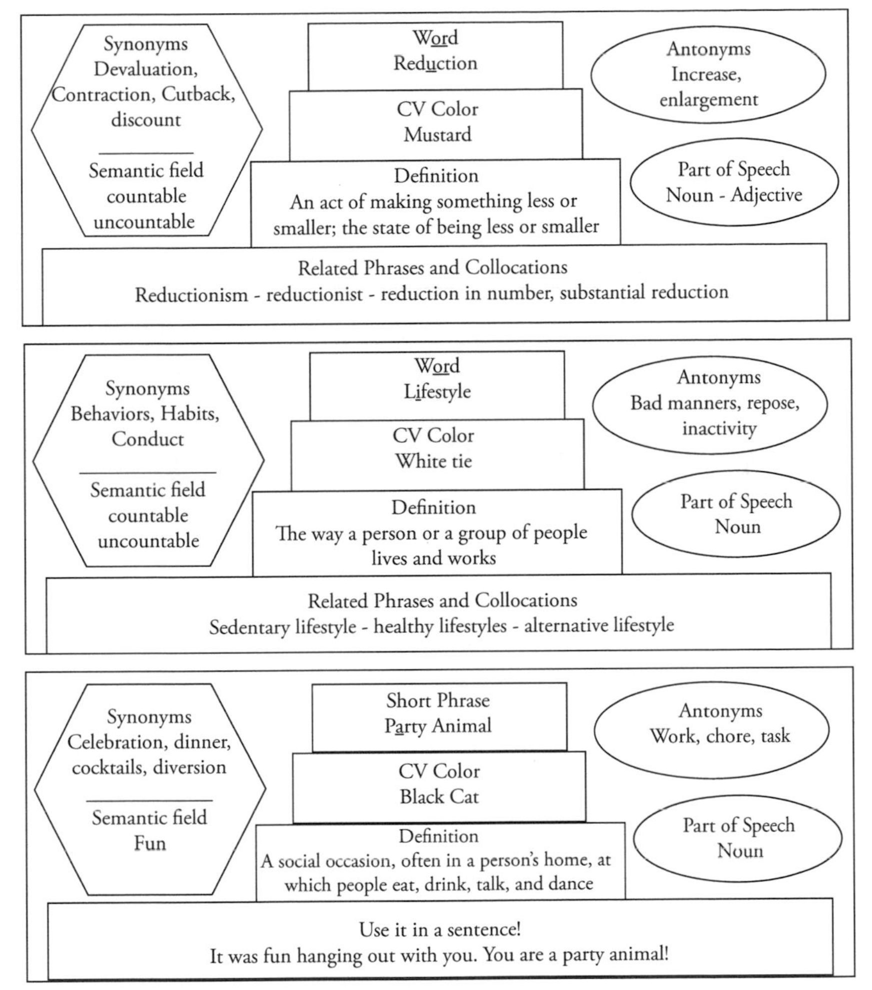

Figure 4.3 Professor Zak Radd's Word Cloud Organizer

Figure 4.4 Level 6 Mind-Map Example 1

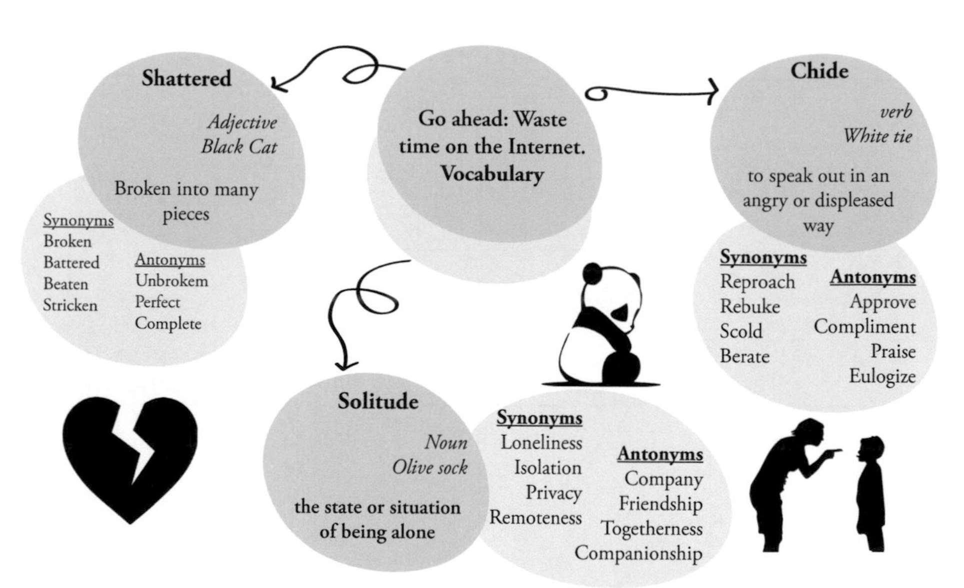

Figure 4.5 Level 6 Mind-Map Example 2

3. Extensive Reading Finale

✓ Levels A1 to C1
✓ Online compatible

Grabe and Yamashita (2022) make the excellent point that extensive reading is fundamental to recursive encounters with vocabulary and syntax. The idea is not to deliberately "teach" the book or novel, but let students engage in reading for pleasure, if not outside the classroom, then at least for 30 to 45 minutes each week within the classroom. Additionally, listening to an accomplished English speaker read aloud over a period of weeks exposes students to authentic language, rhythm, and intonation. But what do you do once you've reached the end of the book? You want to enable your students to reflect on their reading experience and talk about plot, character, language, and whether they enjoyed the text and why!

Link to Theory:

An **extensive reading finale** task serves to:

- promote collaborative and communicative engagement;
- prompt close reading and textual analysis;
- practice summary and paraphrase;
- prompt critical thinking skills;
- promote linguistic awareness.

Procedure:

1. Divide your class into groups of three or four students.
2. Provide each group with a different section, chapter, character, or important plot event.
3. Instruct the group to create an attractive PowerPoint slide with a summary or description of "their" chapter, event, character. Instruct students to explain the importance of their section, chapter, character, etc., to the overall text: does it move the plot forward, create tension, create resolution? How is the character key to the plot or theme?
4. Provide each group with a relevant quote from their chapter, section, plot event, character, or for higher levels, ask students to identify a relevant quote. Ask them to annotate the quote for:
    a. emotive language, expressive verbs, adjectives, adverbs;
    b. sentence types and how they build tension, provide information, reveal the character's state of mind.

5. Provide time in class to plan the presentation, gather information, and analyze language.
6. Hold group presentations and award points for completion, diligence, and quality of analysis.

Example of Extensive Reading Finale

Novel: ***Coraline***

CEFR level: B1

Figure 4.6 gives an example of the extensive reading finale exercise based on the Neil Gaiman novel *Coraline*.

Stages 1–3: Students are placed in small groups of three to four students to discuss the exercise, follow the instructions and consider the general questions on character and plot...

Stage 4: The groups look at the quote from *Coraline* and analyze it together following the instructions.

Stage 5–6: Figure 4.7 shows an example of language analysis in process and this will form the basis of the group's presentation of the completed analysis of language elements, character and plot to the class which the instructor will assess.

B1 Group Work: 10-minute presentation
Character *Coraline.*
Create a PowerPoint or poster to illuminate your presentation.

1. Who is Coraline? Describe the character and explain why she is important to the plot.
2. What key events involve Coraline?
3. What does the quote below tell us about Coraline and how she feels?
   "Coraline shivered. She preferred her other mother to have a location: if she were nowhere, then she could be anywhere. And, after all, it is always easier to be afraid of something you cannot see."
4. Analyze the quote for interesting verbs, adjectives, adverbs, and nouns.
5. What sentence types can you identify in this quote? Why do you think the author uses these sentence types?
6. Did you enjoy the novel? Explain.

Figure 4.6 Extensive Reading Finale Task

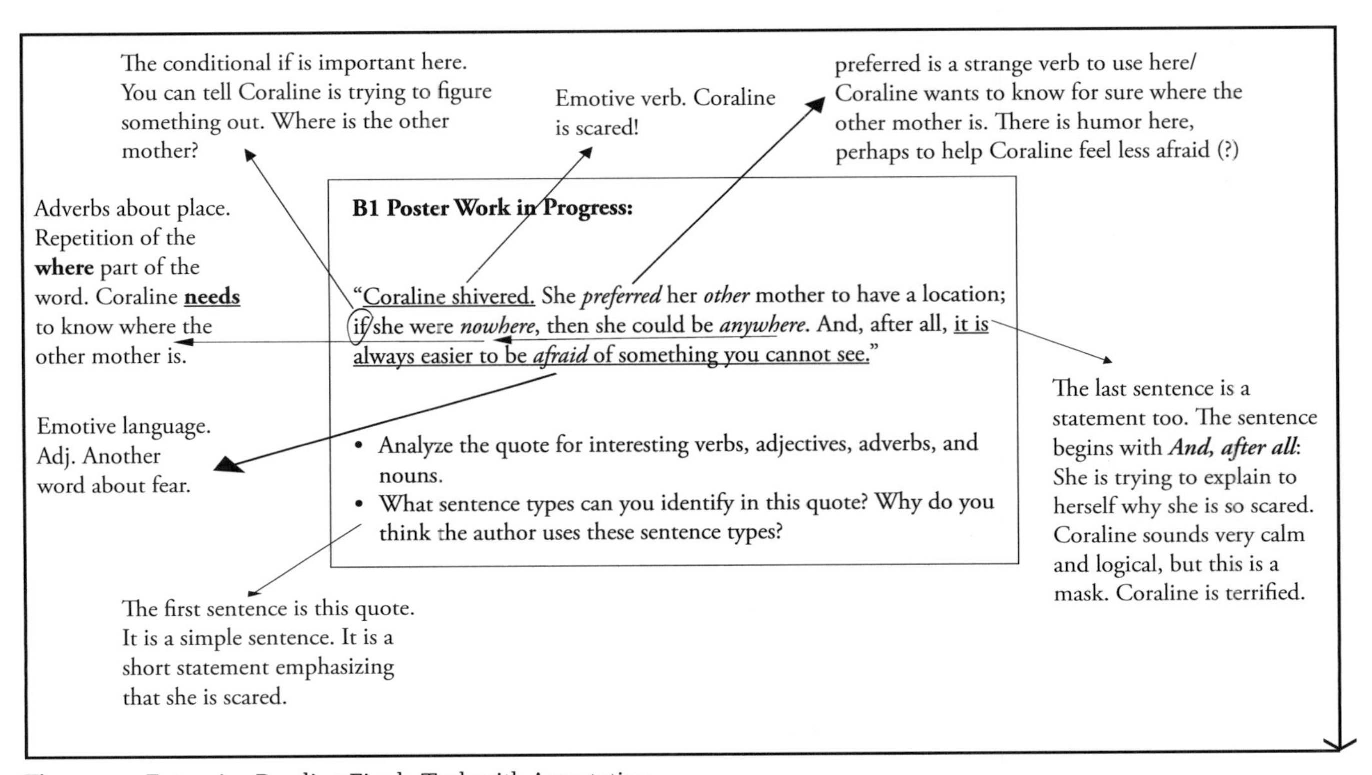

The conditional if is important here. You can tell Coraline is trying to figure something out. Where is the other mother?
Emotive verb. Coraline is scared!
preferred is a strange verb to use here/ Coraline wants to know for sure where the other mother is. There is humor here, perhaps to help Coraline feel less afraid (?)
Adverbs about place. Repetition of the where part of the word. Coraline needs to know where the other mother is.
B1 Poster Work in Progress:
"Coraline shivered. She preferred her other mother to have a location; if she were nowhere, then she could be anywhere. And, after all, it is always easier to be afraid of something you cannot see."
Emotive language. Adj. Another word about fear.
• Analyze the quote for interesting verbs, adjectives, adverbs, and nouns.
• What sentence types can you identify in this quote? Why do you think the author uses these sentence types?
The last sentence is a statement too. The sentence begins with And, after all: She is trying to explain to herself why she is so scared. Coraline sounds very calm and logical, but this is a mask. Coraline is terrified.
The first sentence is this quote. It is a simple sentence. It is a short statement emphasizing that she is scared.

Figure 4.7 Extensive Reading Finale Task with Annotation

This activity can be adapted for all levels. FAU IEI A1 students are currently reading Dr. Seuss' *The Sneetches* and A2 to C1 are currently reading graded readers on crime, romance, and adventure. Any fiction text can be analyzed for interesting verbs and adjectives, character development, plot structure, and authorial viewpoint. Students at any level can read, enjoy, expand linguistic awareness, and express an opinion on content. In order to grow automaticity and fluency, students have to read or be read to. As always, this is an interactive process and students engage language awareness without realizing they are doing so.

4. Pre-Reading Activities Reframed to Post-Reading Activities

✓ Levels A1 to C1
✓ Online compatible

- Revisit your thunk, or pose a new one after reading the text in class. Has the text changed student responses? Could they pose their own thunk after reading the text?
- Revisit *Morning Prompts* after reading the text and hold a discussion on *if* and *how* the text has changed student attitudes. Would they have responded differently to the Morning Prompt if they had read the text first? Would they consider a different Morning Prompt more appropriate? What would they suggest?
- Revisit the *four-corners debate* to see if students' positions change post-reading; discuss any changes, or lack of changes. How difficult was it for students to commit to a position; how do they feel about their position post-reading?
- *Hot-seat* a "character" or "author" from your text and instruct the "audience" to compose questions on authorial stance and content: What made the "author" write the article/text/novel? Why did they choose a particular structure to convey their message? Why did they choose particular vocabulary? What do they expect readers to do once they have read the text?
- Revisit your *Diamond Sequence*: would your students change their sequence post-reading? If so, how and why?

Pre-reading activities can be revisited to consolidate vocabulary, grammar, encourage post-reading critical appraisal of content and authorial viewpoint. Framing a text with pre-reading, interactive reading, and post-reading activities provides a solid preview, overview, and afterview of text. Providing schemata, reducing volume, and contextualizing post-reading promotes critical thinking skills and enables students to grapple with reading skills with cognitive burden firmly under control.

Chapter 5

Adapting Activities to Digital Platforms

I am not a digital native! I handwrote my English literature essays during first and second year of undergraduate studies and used a Brother electric typewriter for year 3. I familiarized myself with Word, Excel, PowerPoint, and Photoshop in my late twenties and early thirties during graduate studies, and viewed the younger digital natives with envy as their hands flew effortlessly over keyboards to create both written content and stunning images. I did, however, keep pace with basic technology as I began my teaching career and passed the compulsory teachers' technology test. I didn't *mind* technology in the classroom, but I was fine with my overhead projector and smartboard; anything more seemed unnecessarily burdensome.

Covid-19, however, brought about a tectonic shift in our perception of what *can* be done online. With necessity the mother of invention, even reluctant technophobes like myself moved classes online and began to use Webex, Google Docs, and Zoom as if they were born to the screen rather than dragged there weeping due to an ongoing worldwide health crisis. Previously unfamiliar with online digital platforms, I moved our entire program online over one weekend, trained my instructors in synchronous and asynchronous teaching and learning in the space of a two-hour workshop, hopped between classes once the term began, and viewed online discussion, collaborative learning, and the trials of remotely proctored assessment with a smug sense of accomplishment. I may not be a digital native, but I am definitely a digital migrant and proud to be so!

I learned quite quickly that any in-person activity can be done online. All the activities in chapters 2, 3, and 4 can be adapted to the online environment. Group discussion, individual and group annotation, sequencing activities and hot-seating, jigsaw readings and cloze exercises; all can be done just as well from the comfort of the student's bedroom as from the structure of a bricks and mortar school. Most teachers have their own digital preferences; there are myriad apps and digital tools available for educational use, and it is not possible to list them all! I found the easiest platforms for the activities listed in chapters 2, 3, and 4 are Zoom and Google's Jamboard.

Zoom (https://zoom.us/) enables breakout rooms for pair and group work. It is an excellent tool for online teaching and learning, with cameras on, of course. Zoom's breakout rooms facilitate discussion, and the share option allows students and teacher to share documents and presentations. Annotation tools facilitate highlighting and commentary, and the chat box enables questions and answers, messages, and exchange of information in real time. Just as you'd prepare your PowerPoint presentation and use it on the classroom computer, the same PowerPoint is just as useful online. Just as you'd use a marker to annotate your whiteboard in class, digital annotation tools highlight, underline, circle, and annotate just as well.

Google's Jamboard provides an online whiteboard for collaborative annotation: https://edu.google.com/products/jamboard/ If you are wary, like me, of unfamiliar platforms, a previously unencountered one is enough to quicken the pulse and raise beads of sweat on the forehead. Pothier (2021), however, reassures us that students are familiar with Google products and the program is intuitive. Additionally, Khoiriyah et al. (2022) emphasize students' positive attitude to Jamboard due to its colorful features and collaborative properties. As an online Color Vowel® student myself, I can wholeheartedly support Khoiriyah's statement; I have delighted in moving voiced and voiceless consonants from one part of a slide to another or manipulating post-its with moving and non-moving vowels into categories together with fellow classmates. There are, though, limitations to consider: Zoom and Jamboard are best used on laptops or tablets; mobile phones are less user-friendly. Access to Wi-Fi is also an issue. However, with adequate internet access, appropriate hardware, and with a little preparation by the instructor and allocation of whiteboard slides to individuals or groups, students collaborate, create, and annotate while using Zoom or Jamboard as the classroom. Create your meeting, admit your students, share your Jam of the day, allocate slides to individuals and groups, and get ready, steady, teach!

Conclusion

Reading fluency is defined as smooth, effortless reading and the ability to move beyond automatic word recognition to prosodic features of language (Kuhn & Stahl, 2003). Word recognition, eye tracking resulting in fast reading rate, ability to place words and phrases within clause and sentence level, and phonemic awareness are all key to this process (Grabe & Yamashita, 2022). Aviva's Reading Fluency Flower© (see Figure 6.1) illustrates this process with phonemic awareness at the beginning of the cycle resulting in sound to symbol linkage, orthographic awareness, faster reading rate due to fewer regressions during the physical process of reading, and understanding of morphology and syntax leading to automaticity, which in turn provides more working capacity for thinking skills, and ultimately results in textual comprehension—the construction of meaning from text (Kuhn & Stahl, 2003).

Additionally, reading and writing are bidirectional. Fluent reading skills support writing, and effective writing skills enhance reading (Grabe and Yamashita, 2022; Graham et al., 2018; Graham, 2020). However, while it is easy as an instructor to spend time on productive skills such as writing—we can view grammatical mistakes, syntactic errors, and grade essays for vocabulary, discourse markers, structure, content and register—it is more difficult to teach reading skills and strategies as the internal reading process is not obvious or immediately visible (Singhal, 1998). Without discrete instruction of reading skills, though, reading becomes an uphill climb! The sheer quantity of information on the screen or the page, the navigation of previously unencountered cultural references, and the physiological and mental demands of decoding an L2 create a heavy cognitive burden. It is our responsibility as teachers to reduce this overload and, through continuous exposure to text using pre-reading, interactive reading, and post-reading exercises, promote reading skills and enable access to all that reading in English gifts its readers.

Finally, this book stands on the shoulders of giants. In addition to many others' scholarly work, Grabe and Yamashita's (2022) research provides a comprehensive, updated knowledge of reading in a second language; Maryanne Wolf's beautifully written and insightful books *Proust and the Squid* (2008)

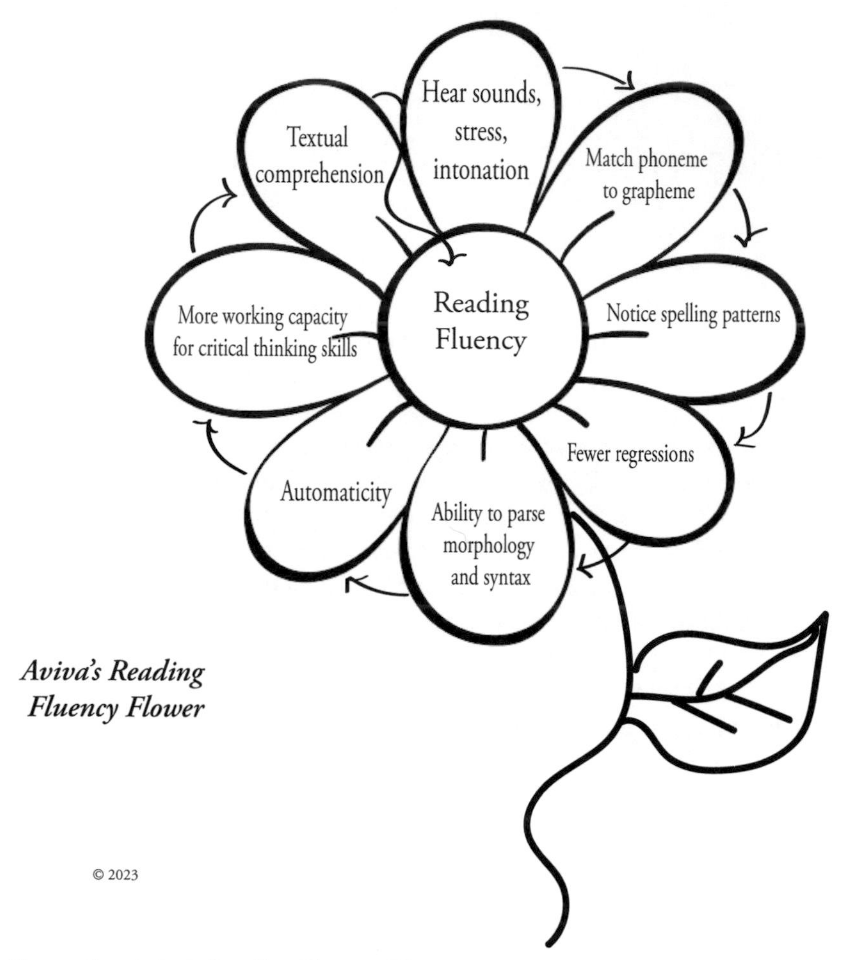

Figure 6.1 Aviva's Reading Fluency Flower

and *Reader, Come Home* (2018) present invaluable information regarding the brain and the history of reading; additionally, Baron, Grabe and Yamashita, and Wolf's discussions on the digital reading landscape and loss of reading skills associated with attention loss make for cautionary reading. Moats and Tolman's (2004) discussion of eye tracking reminds us of the physiological processes involved in reading and provides a timely reminder that reading can be a laborious task; Karen Taylor and Shirley Thompson remind us of the importance of phonemic awareness and how we can utilize the visual, musical, and kinesthetic parts of the brain to hear beyond our L1. Importantly, colleagues and students provide real activities and examples of actual work and put theory into practice.

The real heroes of this book, though, are the students. They are, indeed, "users of information"; they view English as the "end destination," the peak of the mountain, the key to study, work, survival, and integration. Many are overcome by the sheer volume of the written word; many puzzle over cultural references and conventions that we, the culturally aware English readers, take for granted. Our casual stroll through the world of English language takes on a steeper, harsher incline for our students. I hope *Theory and Practice: Bite-sized Activities for Teaching Reading Skills* helps reduce difficulties associated with reading, and provides both instructors and students with pretty vistas, arresting stopping points, and a view of that English language mountain peak with carefully scaffolded steps leading right up to the top.

Thank you to all faculty and students who contributed examples of work to this volume. We can "tell" all we like, but "seeing" is truly believing!

Aviva

GLOSSARY OF KEY TERMS

Anchor phrase: the phrase illustrating a stressed vowel sound in Color Vowel® methodology.

Automaticity: processing that is unconscious, fast, and does not involve working memory space.

Bottom-up processing: processing that is data-driven reading involving letter-by-letter, word-by-word, clause-by-clause; bottom-up processing generally involves lower-order skills.

Elicitation: the act of drawing out information, knowledge, ideas from another person through questions.

Fluency: the ability to read with speed, accuracy, and proper expression.

Freewriting: similar to brainstorming, but written in paragraph format.

Grapheme: a unit of written language that corresponds to a phoneme, a sound of the language.

Jamboard: a digital interactive whiteboard developed by Google.

L1: refers to the first language or mother tongue.

L2: refers to a second language, a language which is not a speaker's mother tongue.

Lexicon: easily accessible vocabulary stored in our long-term memory.

Long-term memory: indefinite storage of information; does not use up working memory capacity.

Orthography: relates to spelling and the written form.

a. Shallow orthography is letter to sound correspondence.

b. Deep orthography shows inconsistencies with letter to sound correspondence. English has a deep orthography.

Phoneme: a sound of the language; changing the sound will change the meaning: /b/at; /r/at; ba/r/; ra/n/

Phonemic awareness: sound awareness considered crucial for reading.

Saccade: fast movement of the eye between fixation points; first language (L1) fixation occurs for approximately 0.25 milliseconds on nouns, verbs, adjectives, and adverbs.

Scaffolding: provides support for learning in order to foster learning independence.

Schema: a means for organizing knowledge in the brain; a mental landscape.

Semantic field: a lexical set of related items. *Jury, lawyer, court, defendant* belong to the semantic field of law.

Top-down processing: knowledge coming from higher-order skills (for example, ability to predict from context; identify theme, abstract concepts, patterns in text).

Working memory: includes the central executive system which coordinates cognitive activity, a short-term visual store, and phonological loop which allows us to store and manipulate spoken and written information.

Zoom: a communications platform enabling users to connect via video, phone, and chat.

REFERENCES

Albay, M. (2017). "The Benefits of Graded Reading." *International Journal of Social Sciences & Educational Studies, 3*(4), 177–180. https://doi.org/10.23918/ijsses.v3i4p17

An, S. (2013). "Schema Theory in Reading." *Theory & Practice in Language Studies, 3*(1), 130–113 doi:10.4304/tpls.3.1.130-134

Ardasheva, Y., Crosson, A. C., Carbonneau, K. J., & French, B. F. (2021). "Unpacking contributions of morphosyntactic awareness and vocabulary to science reading comprehension among Linguistically diverse students." *TESOL Quarterly*, 55(3), 931–965.

Austen, J. (1995). *Favorite Jane Austen novels: Complete and unabridged.* Dover Publications.

Baddeley, A. (2007). *Working memory, thought, and action* (Vol. 45). OUP Oxford.

Baron, N. S. (2021). *How we read now: Strategic choices for print, screen, and audio.* Oxford University Press.

Blue Canoe Learning. (2018, October 31). *The Complete Color Vowel Chart* [Video]. YouTube. https://www.youtube.com/watch?v=9PB_3JPFbGY

Burt, M., Peyton, J. K., & Adams, R. (2003). Reading and adult English language learners: A review of the research. *National Center for ESL Literacy Education (NCLE).*

Council of Europe. (2020). *Common European Framework of Reference for Languages: Learning, Teaching, Assessment – Companion Volume.* Council of Europe Publishing, Strasbourg. https://www.coe.int/en/web/common-european-framework-reference-languages/uses-and-objectives

Ellis, N. C. (1996). "Working memory in the acquisition of vocabulary and syntax: Putting language in good order." *The Quarterly Journal of Experimental Psychology Section A, 49*(1): 234–250.

Gibbons, P. (2015). *Scaffolding language, scaffolding learning.* 2nd ed. Portsmouth, NH: Heinemann.

Gilbert, I. (2007). *The little book of thunks: 260 questions to make your brain go ouch!* Crown House.

Grabe, W. (2014). Key issues in L2 reading development. In *Proceedings of the 4th CELC Symposium for English Language Teachers-Selected Papers* (pp. 8–18).

Grabe, W. and Yamashita, J. (2022). *Reading in a second language: Moving from theory to practice*. Cambridge University Press.

Graham, S., Liu, X., Bartlett, B., Ng, C., Harris, K. R., Aitken, A., Barkel, A., Kavanaugh, C., & Talukdar, J. (2018). "Reading for writing: A meta-analysis of the impact of reading interventions on writing. *Review of Educational Research, 88*(2): 243–284. https://doi.org/10.3102/0034654317746927

Graham, S. (2020). "The sciences of reading and writing must become more fully integrated." *Reading Research Quarterly*, 55, S35S44. https://doi.org/10.1002/rrq.332

Horn, T, Downes, G, & Woolley, B. in 1978. Itl (1979). Video Killed the Radio Star [Recorded by B, Woolley]. On album *English Garden.*

Khoiriyah, K., Kairoty, N., & Aljasysyarin, A. V. (2022). "The use of Google Jamboard for synchronous collaborative reading strategies: The students' acceptance." *VELES: Voices of English Language Education Society*, 6(1), 52–66. https://doi.org/10.29408/veles.v6i1.5010.

Kuhn, M. R., and Stahl, S. A. (2003). "Fluency: A review of developmental and remedial practices." *Journal of Educational Psychology*, 95(1): 3–21. https://doi.org/10.1037/0022-0663.95.1.3.

Laufer, B., and Ravenhorst-Kalovski, G. C. (2010). "Lexical threshold revisited: Lexical text coverage, learners' vocabulary size and reading comprehension." *Reading in a Foreign Language*, 22(1): 15–30.

Moats, L. C., & Tolman, C. (2004). *Language essentials for teachers of reading and spelling*. Longmont, CO: Sopris West Educational Services.

Nation, I. (2022). The Cambridge Applied Linguistics Series. In *Learning Vocabulary in Another Language* (Cambridge Applied Linguistics, pp. ii-iv). Cambridge University Press.

Nation, P. & Wang, K. (1999). Graded Readers and Vocabulary. Open Access Te Herenga Waka-Victoria University of Wellington. Journal contribution. https://doi.org/10.26686/wgtn.12560366.v1.

Nisbet, K., Bertram, R., Erlinghagen, C., Pieczykolan, A., & Kuperman, V. (2021). "Quantifying the difference in reading fluency between L1 and L2 readers of English." *Studies in Second Language Acquisition*, 44(2): 407–434. doi:10.1017/S0272263121000279

Park, H. (2018). "The role of reading span in L2 reading comprehension and eye movements." *English Teaching*, 73(1): 3–21. https://doi.org/10.15858/engtea.73.1.201803.3.

Pothier, W. (2021). "Jamming together: Concept mapping in the pandemic classroom." *Ticker: The Academic Business Librarianship Review*, 5 (2). https://doi.org/10.3998/ticker.16481003.0005.220.

Roberts, L, and Siyanova-Chanturia, A. (2021). "Using eye-tracking to investigate topics in L2 acquisition and L2 sentence and discourse processing." https://doi.org/10.26686/wgtn.13670659.v1.

Short, D., Becker, H., Cloud, N., & Hellman, A. B. (2018). *The 6 principles for exemplary teaching of English learners: Grades K-12*. TESOL Press.

Singhal, M. (1998). "A comparison of L1 and L2 reading: Cultural differences and schema." *The Internet TESL Journal, 4*(10).

Smith, R., Snow, P., Serry, T., & Hammond, L. (2021). "The role of background knowledge in reading comprehension: A critical review." *Reading Psychology, 42*(3): 214–240.

Snowling,M.J.,&Hulme,C.E.(2005).*Thescienceofreading:Ahandbook*.Blackwell Publishing. 214–240. https://doi.org/10.1080/02702711.2021.1888348.

Stanovich, K. E. (2009). "Matthew effects in reading: Some consequences of individual differences in the acquisition of literacy." *Journal of Education, 189*(1–2): 23–55.

Sweet, A. P., & Snow, C. E. (Eds.). (2003). *Rethinking reading comprehension*. Guilford Press.

Taylor, K. (2020). *Color Vowel® Basics | English Language Course*. English Language Training Solutions. https://learn.colorvowel.com/courses/basics

Taylor, K. (2021). *Sound Awareness. Revolutionize English Language Teaching and Learning*. https://learn.colorvowel.com/courses/lvl2-awareness

Taylor, K., & Thompson, S. (2018). *The color vowel chart*. Santa Fe, NM: English Language Training Solutions.

Taylor,K.,Thompson,S.,&Barr,R.(2016).TheColorVowelapproach:Resources for connecting pronunciation to vocabulary, reading, and spelling.

Trenité, G. N. (n.d.). *The Chaos*. https://people.cs.georgetown.edu/nschneid/cosc272/f17/a1/chaos.html

The COLOR VOWEL Organizer © 2019 English Language Training Solutions, Santa Fe, NM.

Wolf, M. (2008). *Proust and the squid: The story and science of the reading brain*. New York: Harper Perennial.

Wolf, M. (2018). *Reader, come home: The reading brain in a digital world*. New York: Harper.

Young, C., & Nageldinger, J. (2014). "Considering the context and texts for fluency: Performance, readers theater, and poetry." *International Electronic Journal of Elementary Education, 7*(1): 47–56.